Level 10

Authors
Matthew Stephens
Athena Lester
Danielle Nettleton

Designer
Boston Stephens

Permissions
Sherri Gilbert

Consultant
Molly Lasater

Project Coordinator
Athena Lester

Editors
Athena Lester
Danielle Nettleton

417-256-4191
www.essentialsinliterature.com
Copyright © 2017 by Matthew B. Stephens

All rights reserved. No part of this book may be reproduced, or transmitted in any form by any means - electronic, mechanical, photocopying, recording or otherwise.

Printed in the United States of America
Update January 2022

TABLE OF CONTENTS

Fiction 4
   Bernice Bobs Her Hair 15
   Amigo Brothers 21
   The Necklace 27
   Harrison Bergeron 33
   The Yellow Wallpaper 39
   The Speckled Band 45
   A Worn Path 51
   Summative Assessment 57

Drama 58
   Trifles 71
   The Boor 77
   Summative Assessment 83
   Culminating Activity 84

Novel: To Kill a Mockingbird 88
   Section One 91
   Section Two 95
   Section Three 99
   Section Four 103
   Section Five 107
   Section Six 111
   Summative Assessment 115
   Culminating Activity 116

Poetry 120
   Introduction to Poetry & A Loaf of Poetry 131
   If– & Women 135
   Are You Digging on My Grave? & Go and Catch a Falling Star 139
   One Art & How Do I Love Thee? 143
   Having a Coke with You & [in Just-] 147
   Summative Assessment 151

Fiction Unit

The Literature You'll Read:

F. Scott Fitzgerald	Bernice Bobs Her Hair
Piri Thomas	Amigo Brothers
Guy de Maupassant	The Necklace
Kurt Vonnegut	Harrison Bergeron
Charlotte Perkins Gilman	The Yellow Wallpaper
Sir Arthur Conan Doyle	The Speckled Band
Eudora Welty	A Worn Path
Katherine Mansfield	*A Doll's House

The Concepts You'll Study:

Analyzing Literature
Protagonist/Antagonist
Characters (Dynamic/Static; Flat/Round)
Motivation
Conflict (Internal and External)
Theme
Irony
Satire
Mood
Symbolism
Point of View
Foreshadowing

Vocabulary
Denotative vs. Connotative meaning
Foreign words
Synonyms
Archaic words
Association

Summative Assessment

Reading Focus
Making Connections
Making Predictions
Visualize
Compare and Contrast
Drawing Conclusions
Monitor

Writing Connection
Narrative
Personal Journal
Letter
Newspaper Article
Writing from a Fictional Point of View
Poetry

Nonfiction Connection
Articles
History
Encyclopedia Entry
Biographies
Film Reviews

Exploring Literature  Day 1

Fiction

Humanity communicates with each other through stories. Every ancient culture used stories to explain natural phenomena they did not scientifically understand, such as why the sun moves through the sky and why the seasons change. When explorers traveled to new lands and returned home, they shared their experiences and findings through stories.

A work of fiction is an imagined account of people (**characters**), places (**settings**), and events (**plots**) that communicates something valuable or important to real life.

Fiction Genres

Realistic Fiction
- events, characters, and settings mirroring the real world

Science Fiction
- plots that revolve around futuristic science and technology

Mystery
- puzzling elements (often crimes) that must be solved

Fantasy
- realistically impossible elements, such as magic and talking animals

Historical Fiction
- imagined characters and plots in a factual setting from the past, interacting with real events

Traditional
- fairytales and myths passed down through generations

Works of fiction that can be read in one sitting are called **short stories**, which focus on simple plots and a single idea. Longer works that have complicated plots, many characters, and more intricate themes are called **novels**. Works that are longer than most short stories but are not long enough to be novels are called **novellas**.

The opposite of fiction is **nonfiction**, prose writing based on factual events and real people. Types of nonfiction include **articles**, **biographies**, and **historical accounts**.

Plot

While some stories are essentially plotless (such as Ernest Hemingway's "Hills Like White Elephants"), most narratives contain a **plot**—a series of events that revolves around a central **conflict**. Plot and conflict are closely intertwined because the plot records characters' actions to resolve the conflict.

Sometimes, in addition to the main plot, stories contain **subplots**, a small story arc contained within a larger one. Subplots often support the main plot indirectly and complicate the central conflict.

> *In Alexander Dumas' novel* The Three Musketeers, *the plot focuses on young d'Artagnan in his quest to keep the Queen of France safe. A subplot of the novel, however, involves d'Artagnan's attempts to win the heart of a young woman named Constance. Even though the arc is part of the story, this subplot is not the main focus.*

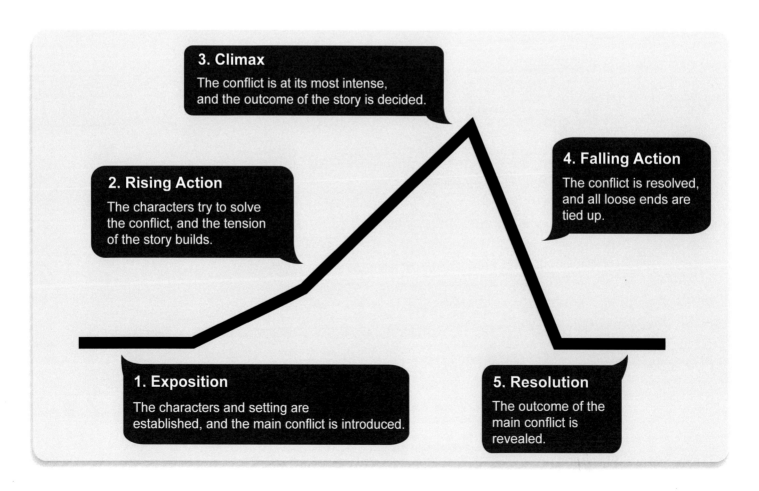

1. **Exposition** — The characters and setting are established, and the main conflict is introduced.
2. **Rising Action** — The characters try to solve the conflict, and the tension of the story builds.
3. **Climax** — The conflict is at its most intense, and the outcome of the story is decided.
4. **Falling Action** — The conflict is resolved, and all loose ends are tied up.
5. **Resolution** — The outcome of the main conflict is revealed.

Conflict

What's the point of reading a story where everything is perfect and the characters encounter no problems? Readers gravitate toward **conflict** in tales—a struggle between opposing forces. Conflict keeps readers engaged in the plot because they want to know how the problems are resolved. Conflict also invests readers in the characters because they want to see how the characters will respond to the struggle.

In literature, conflict is divided into two main categories: **external conflict** and **internal conflict**. These categories, however, can be subdivided even further.

A piece of literature can have multiple types of conflict within the same work. Often, external conflict reflects a character's internal conflict.

External Conflict
A character struggles against an outside force

Person vs. Person	A character struggles against another human being, such as a parent, a supervillain, or a bully
Person vs. Nature	A character struggles against some kind of natural element, such as a hot desert, a tornado, or a pack of wolves
Person vs. Society	A character struggles with an intangible element of their culture, such as laws, religion, or traditions

Internal Conflict

	A character struggles inside their own heart or mind, often as the result of fear, contrasting desires, or emotional trauma

In The Adventures of Huckleberry Finn *by Mark Twain, Huck and his friend Jim—a runaway slave—clash with other people and society. The story's antagonists want to sell Jim back into slavery, and Huck and Jim live in a society that does not value Jim as a human being because he is black.*

At the same time, Huck must choose between what society thinks is right and what he thinks is right—that is, selling Jim back into slavery or keeping him safe. Huck also struggles with how he is supposed to view Jim—as a lesser being (for that is what society tells him) or as his friend (for that is how Huck has come to feel about Jim). The external conflict Huck faces reflects and emphasizes this internal conflict.

FICTION

Characters

Plot revolves around characters' actions, and conflict revolves around characters' struggles. **Main characters** are central to a plot and vital to the central conflict, while *minor characters* move the plot along but are not fundamental to the story.

In the Pirates of the Caribbean *movies, Captain Jack Sparrow is the protagonist of the story, but he is also a thief, a liar, and a drunk. He is the focus, but he is not a hero.*

Main characters can be protagonists or antagonists. A **protagonist** is the focus of a story because the plot follows their actions, and an **antagonist** opposes the protagonist in a conflict. Sometimes a protagonist is called a hero, but the protagonist is not always a good person.

When studying fiction, special categories can be useful when analyzing characters. These categories are *dynamic*, *static*, *flat*, and *round*. Main characters are almost always round, but minor characters can be round or flat. Generally—but not always—main characters are also dynamic in some way.

Dynamic Character
A dynamic character changes during the course of a story. Their emotions, actions, or mindsets undergo some kind of transformation.

Static Character
A static character does not change. They remain the same person at the end of the story as they were at the beginning.

Flat Character
A flat character is uncomplicated, and the reader learns very little about them. They are sometimes used to simply move the plot along.

Round Character
A round character is developed and complex. A reader gets to know them, their past, thoughts, and feelings in depth.

Traits and Motives

Characters are defined by their traits.
traits: defining qualities, characteristics, and personality features

Characters are driven by their motives.
motives: reasons characters take certain actions

Setting

When and where a story takes place is called the **setting**. Sometimes setting can impact the plot and conflict of a piece of fiction, but not always.

Temporal setting involves the time in which a story takes place. This kind of setting includes dates in the past, present, or future as well as seasons and the time of day.

Chinese New Year
March 15, 44 B.C.

Trenches in France
A plane over the Atlantic Ocean

Physical setting involves the location in which a story takes place. This kind of setting revolves around physical places, including everything from a particular room in a house to an entire planet and everything in between.

These two aspects of setting work together to create the overall setting of a story. Readers understand the setting of a work through descriptions in the narration as well as through characters' actions and speech. Can you recognize what kind of setting these characters are in based on their words?

"Y'all come back by supper, ya hear? And don't go by Akins' Creek neither. Mr. Jethro's in a bad way and don't need no disturbances."

"The subway shut down and I couldn't find a cab to save my life. By then I was already late, so I went by the deli to grab a bagel."

"No, I can't upgrade to the new holoscreen. I'm saving every last credit I can so I can buy passage off this lousy planet someday."

FICTION

Point of View

The perspective from which a story is told is called its **point of view**. Most stories are told in **third-person perspective** or **first-person perspective**.

Third Person

The story is told from a narrator not directly involved in the plot. The narrator uses third person pronouns to tell the story.

Third person omniscient
The narrator has access to all characters' inner workings as well as outer actions. This point of view knows everything there is to know about everyone in the story. A story told in this perspective is not very suspenseful because no knowledge is withheld; however, the author has the chance to explicitly communicate anything they wish to the reader.

In The Octopus by Frank Norris, the narration includes the internal emotions, thoughts, and motivations of every character, emphasizing the overall purpose of the novel: revealing the impact and intricacies of large communities.

Third person limited
The narrator only has access to select characters' inner workings. The narrator knows everything there is to know about only certain characters. This limited perspective allows the narrator to intimately reveal a character to the reader but still make judgments on the character's actions or thoughts, calling them wise or foolish or something else.

Henry James' novel The American focuses on a man involved with an aristocratic family with a dark secret. The man attempts to uncover this secret to serve his own purposes, and the reader only learns the truth when he does, all the while judging whether or not his own actions are justified.

Objective
The narrator reveals only outward actions and events, revealing no internal thoughts or feelings whatsoever. This narrator is almost like a video camera, only describing external things. The narration makes no judgments on what occurs and never provides any of the characters' internal reasoning, thus allowing the reader to process the story on their own.

Ernest Hemingway's short story "Hills Like White Elephants" is mostly dialogue with no indication as to what the conversation means. The narration allows the reader to observe the characters in the story like one would observe real people—without any access to internal workings.

First Person

The story is told through a narrator who is directly involved in the plot. The narration includes personal pronouns like *I, we, my,* and *our* and reveals all the information, thoughts, and feelings of only the narrating character. When a story is told in first person point of view, the information presented to readers is filtered through the character's mind and may not be entirely accurate or reliable.

The Hunger Games by Suzanne Collins is narrated directly by the main character Katniss. The reader knows only what Katniss knows, and she does not know everything that happens in her world or to other characters. The reader has to wade through Katniss's internal dialogue in order to piece together the entire story.

Foreshadowing and Flashback

Foreshadowing is a warning or indication of a future event. In literature, foreshadowing hints at what is to come. Usually, readers do not understand foreshadowing elements until they read the work a second time.

> *In Dickens' A Tale of Two Cities, the courtroom trial near the beginning in which Sydney Carton reveals that he and Charles Darnay look identical foreshadows the end of the book, where another trial takes place and the identicality of the men comes into play. The reader, however, is unaware of this foreshadowing unless they already know how the story ends.*

While foreshadowing looks forward in a story, a **flashback** looks backwards. Flashbacks are moments when characters remember an event that occurred earlier in the story or even before the story began. Authors use flashbacks to reveal information about the past or to remind the reader of something important.

> *Near the beginning of The Outsiders by S.E. Hinton, the narrating character Ponyboy relates how his friend Johnny was once severely beaten by a rival gang. Rather than only stating that the event happened, Ponyboy's flashback interrupts the plot of the book to narrate the situation with details and actions.*

 Day 5

Irony

Irony is a contrast or inconsistency between expectations and reality. Something in literature is ironic when what occurs is different than what the reader or the characters expected.

A family spends months diligently preparing for a beautiful outdoor wedding, complete with exquisite flower arrangements, linen seat coverings, and a rose-covered aisle for the bride to walk down. On the day of the wedding, however, the weather turns sour and pours down seven inches of rain.	A secret agent doesn't tell her husband that she is a spy, for she is afraid her job will ruin their marriage. She lies about where she goes on long trips and what she does with her time. Her husband eventually discovers that she is not being honest. He divorces her because he cannot trust her anymore.	A businessman's alarm clock doesn't go off one morning, so he wakes up late. He spills coffee on his white shirt as he rushes out the door so he has to go back and change. When he finally gets on the road—already half an hour late—he finds bumper-to-bumper traffic all the way to his office building.

Only one of these scenarios is truly *ironic*. The first and the third scenarios are unfortunate, and events occur that the characters did not desire, but they are not ironic. In the second example, however, the secret agent expected her activities as a spy to ruin her marriage, so she told lies intended to preserve her relationship with her husband. In the end, her lies—not her job—are what destroy her marriage. This contrast between her expectations and what actually occurred demonstrates irony.

situational irony
The secret agent told lies to preserve her marriage, but her act of lying destroyed it.

When the outcome of a situation is different than what is expected.

dramatic irony
The reader knows that the owner of a hotel is a killer, but the heroes do not know, so they book a room.

When the audience knows something the characters do not know.

verbal irony
A blind detective finally solves a mystery, and he says, "I see everything clearly now."

When something a character says is different than what they mean.

Mood

The *mood* of a work of fiction is the prevalent emotion that a reader feels while reading the story. Literature can have a depressing mood, a cheerful mood, a suspenseful mood, a frightening mood, or any number of adjectives to describe its mood. Mood is not entirely dependent on subject matter but is dependent on how the subject matter is treated through descriptions of the setting, characters, dialogue, and other story elements.

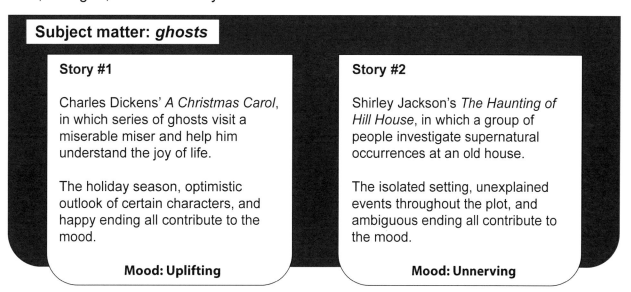

Subject matter: *ghosts*

Story #1

Charles Dickens' *A Christmas Carol*, in which series of ghosts visit a miserable miser and help him understand the joy of life.

The holiday season, optimistic outlook of certain characters, and happy ending all contribute to the mood.

Mood: Uplifting

Story #2

Shirley Jackson's *The Haunting of Hill House*, in which a group of people investigate supernatural occurrences at an old house.

The isolated setting, unexplained events throughout the plot, and ambiguous ending all contribute to the mood.

Mood: Unnerving

Tone

In contrast to mood, *tone* is an author's attitude toward their own story. Does the author treat their subject matter seriously or flippantly? Are they emotional or distant? What is described positively and negatively? The tone of a work determines the answers to these questions. Two stories can contain similar subject matter but be written with vastly different tones.

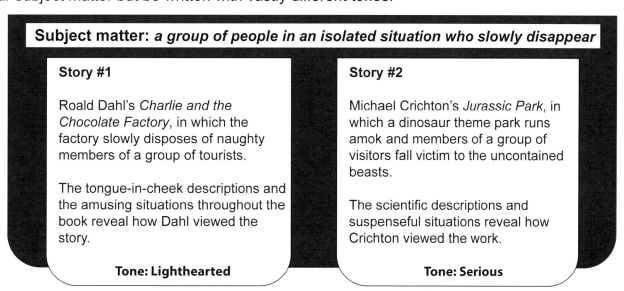

Subject matter: *a group of people in an isolated situation who slowly disappear*

Story #1

Roald Dahl's *Charlie and the Chocolate Factory*, in which the factory slowly disposes of naughty members of a group of tourists.

The tongue-in-cheek descriptions and the amusing situations throughout the book reveal how Dahl viewed the story.

Tone: Lighthearted

Story #2

Michael Crichton's *Jurassic Park*, in which a dinosaur theme park runs amok and members of a group of visitors fall victim to the uncontained beasts.

The scientific descriptions and suspenseful situations reveal how Crichton viewed the work.

Tone: Serious

FICTION

Symbolism

Symbolism is the use of a person, place, object, or action to express a deeper or double meaning, often describing an idea or concept that has no physical attributes. Symbolism creates at least two levels of meaning. One is the literal meaning that applies only to the plot of the story. The other level of meaning is the symbolic meaning, which applies beyond the immediate situation, leading to widely applicable themes.

Symbols in literature can appear for only a fleeting moment, or they can reoccur throughout an entire work.

> In Elie Wiesel's Night, at one point during the Jewish prisoners' nightmare-like experience in the Nazi concentration camps, someone finds a violin and plays a song during the darkest part of the night. This music in the midst of suffering is an individual symbol of hope.

> A symbol that pervades an entire work is found in Peter Pan by J. M. Barrie. The titular character symbolizes childhood, for he never grows up and everything is a game to him. Everything Peter Pan does in the story points to his role as a symbol—his desire for a mother, his belief in fantastical things like fairies, and his carefree nature that allows him to fly.

Certain symbols have been used repeatedly in literature and are easy to identify, although some works may use symbols in a new or fresh way.

- **the color red** — anger or love
- **covering one's eyes** — fear or shame
- **love** — goodness or knowledge
- **snakes** — evil or cunning

Theme

Theme is a pervasive meaning woven throughout a piece of literature. Theme cannot be adequately expressed in one or two words (like *true love* or *courage*); rather, theme is always expressed in a full sentence (such as *True love conquers all* or *Courage gives one the strength to overcome difficulty*). Themes can be lessons or instructions to the reader, or they may simply be observations about life.

Sometimes, themes in stories are obvious. A character or the narrator may explicitly state the theme. Other times, theme is very subtle, and the reader needs to read the story very closely to understand its overall meaning. Repeated elements, symbols, and what is portrayed positively and negatively in a work can all help reveal a story's theme. Other places to find theme are:

- the story's title
- how the conflict is resolved
- character's thoughts, actions, and words
- the lesson a character learns

Bernice Bobs Her Hair

 Day 1: Before You Read

It's all about Popular!

WHAT TO LEARN?

- Protagonist and Antagonist
- Making Connections
- Article
- Independent Practice

American Literature

How far would you go to be popular? Some people naturally fit in wherever they are; others may find that blending in requires effort. Whether in high school or later on in life, the desire to be part of the in-crowd can be overwhelming.

Consider the song "Popular" from the musical *Wicked* or Princess Mia's makeover in the movie *The Princess Diaries*. In each case, someone is telling unpopular characters that in order to be liked by others, they must change who they are, at least superficially.

The process of fitting in usually requires more than a movie montage; in fact, some people may find that the price of popularity is more than they are willing to pay, especially if they are asked to abandon their values or beliefs. The lure of popularity, however, is often too tempting to resist.

How do you feel about cliques or in-crowds? Have you ever changed something about yourself in order to fit in better? How did you feel about this change? Discuss your answer with your teacher or fellow students.

Meet the Author — F. Scott Fitzgerald

Louise Lobs Her Locks

The story "Bernice Bobs Her Hair" is loosely based on letters Fitzgerald sent to his sister Louise advising her how to be more appealing to the young men around her. Whether or not this advice was actually sought by Louise is less certain.

A Man of His Times

One of the most influential writers of the Jazz Age, Fitzgerald focused his novels and short stories around the shifting society of 1920s America. He chronicled the triumphs and despair of this new culture.

Sep 24, 1896–Dec 21, 1940

FICTION 15

Day 2: Before You Read

Analyzing Literature — Protagonist and Antagonist

The word *protagonist* is a combination of the Greek words for "first in order" and "actor." A protagonist, then, is the actor (or character) who is most important in the story. The word *antagonist* comes from the Greek word for "struggle against," so the antagonist struggles against the protagonist. The word "antagonize" comes from the same Greek word.

A hero can be and is often the protagonist, but the protagonist is not always a hero. The protagonist is simply the focus of the story, and they may exhibit positive or negative qualities, motives, and actions.

Modern realistic fiction (such as "Bernice Bobs Her Hair") tends to use protagonists who are not heroes. This does not mean that the protagonists are not good people but rather that they are imperfect characters who make mistakes. In non-fantasy fiction, the protagonist is someone who is relatable to readers, someone who is ordinary.

In the majority of his fiction, F. Scott Fitzgerald presents readers with protagonists who are not only capable of failure but often do fail in some way. In Fitzgerald's *The Great Gatsby*, for example, Jay Gatsby avoids taking responsibility for his actions and blames others instead. Much of Fitzgerald's writing was social commentary; in order to make this commentary, he needed to write realistic characters.

Reading Focus: making connections

"Bernice Bobs Her Hair" features two main characters, the cousins Bernice and Marjorie. As you read, decide which character is more relatable to you. Regardless of your gender, compare yourself to the two characters. Do you sympathize more with Bernice or Marjorie?

Similarities with Bernice	Similarities with Marjorie
I don't feel comfortable talking to people I don't know well.	*I prefer to not let people know how I really feel.*

Reading Focus activity provided in the Resource Book on page 1.

Vocabulary

Words have **denotative** and **connotative** meanings. Denotative refers to the actual definition of the word whereas connotative refers to what people understand the word to mean. Significant changes in denotative meaning rarely occur; connotative meaning, however, often changes. Some of the words and phrases in "Bernice Bobs Her Hair," such as "affair" and "make love," had different connotative meanings in 1920 than they do now. Familiarize yourself with the words listed before you begin reading. Circle words that had different connotative meanings in 1920 and determine when their meanings shifted.

lorgnettes
affair
intimates
pulchritude
histrionic
tonsorial
twitted
bon mot
grip

Read "Bernice Bobs Her Hair" by F. Scott Fitzgerald

 Day 3: After You Read

Check Comprehension

1. **Why** does Bernice finally agree to let Marjorie "coach" her?

2. **Who** is Warren McIntyre?

3. **What** does Bernice do with Marjorie's hair after she cuts it off?

Think Critically

Because "Bernice Bobs Her Hair" is loosely based on letters written to Fitzgerald's sister Louise about how to attract young men, the story could be read as a recommendation to young women of how to behave in society so they will be liked by both men and women. Do you think Fitzgerald intended the story to be read this way, or did he have another purpose in mind? Write an organized paragraph that supports your view with specific details from the story.

After you understand
what happens in a story and
why it happens, ask yourself,
what's the point?

Main Idea

"Bernice Bobs Her Hair" focuses on the relationship between Bernice, the initially awkward cousin from Eau Claire, and Marjorie, the popular socialite who knows how to act around boys and manipulate them to do what she wants. Although Bernice is popular in her hometown, she feels belittled and excluded while visiting Marjorie.

Consider the ultimate reason that Bernice chooses to bob her hair, even though she does not want to, and the numerous clashes between Bernice and Marjorie. What is the main idea of the story, or the most important idea that Fitzgerald wants his readers to take away after finishing the story? Summarize the main idea in one complete sentence.

This story was written in 1920 when bobbing one's hair was still considered scandalous. Short hairstyles for women now are common and do not carry the same implications. Is "Bernice Bobs Her Hair" still relevant in today's society? In one complete sentence, describe in your own words why this story can or cannot be applied to modern readers.

F

Analyzing Literature — Protagonist and Antagonist

The **protagonist** is the focus of a story whereas the **antagonist** opposes the protagonist.

Though the prefixes "pro" and "anta" (or "anti") mean "for" and "against," respectively, keep in mind that the protagonist is not necessarily a good person; they are simply the focus of the story. The categorization of "protagonist" does not always mean that the protagonist is a respectable character that readers should imitate.

Consider the characters of Bernice and Marjorie. Who is the protagonist, and who is the antagonist? Explain your choice for each using supporting examples from the story.

Protagonist: Name here	Antagonist: Name here
Explanation: This character is the protagonist because…	Explanation: This character is the antagonist because…

Analyzing Literature activity provided in the Resource Book on page 2.

DIVE DEEPER

1. **Apply** – In the story, the height of excitement and amusement is the dances given for the young men and women where they can mingle and enjoy each other's company. Plan a social equivalent to these dances today and describe your plan. If an equivalent already exists, what is it? If not, what should be its equivalent?

2. **Analyze** – Both *internal* and *external conflict* are present in the story. Classify an example of each kind of conflict and provide details from the text to support your answers.

3. **Evaluate** – *Situational irony* occurs when what actually happens is the opposite of what was expected. Explain the irony of Bernice cutting her hair to be more popular. Think of the results she expected and compare them to what actually happened.

 Day 4: After You Read

Analyzing Literature

Motive is the reason why characters act the way they do in stories. Just as a locomotive moves from place to place, so a motive moves a character to act.

1. Think about the people and events in "Bernice Bobs Her Hair." What is the main motivation for both Bernice and Marjorie in everything they do?

2. Bernice does not want to bob her hair—she even compares the cutting of her hair to an execution—and knows short hair will not suit her, but she bobs it anyway. What was her motive for cutting her hair, and why was it so strong?

Connection Reflection

3. *"Bernice," she said, "I'm awfully sorry about the Deyo dance. I'll give you my word of honor I'd forgotten all about it."*
Based on her actions, motives, and feelings toward Bernice for the duration of the story, do you think Marjorie truly forgot about the dance and is telling the truth? Why or why not?

4. *"Huh!" she giggled wildly. "Scalp the selfish thing!"*
Consider how Marjorie treats Bernice in the story, especially after Bernice has cut her hair. Was Bernice justified in cutting off Marjorie's hair? How would you have reacted in Bernice's situation? Use details from the text and examples from your own life to support your answers.

Writing Connection

Before Bernice leaves suddenly, she decides to take revenge by cutting off Marjorie's hair and throwing it into Warren's yard. Imagine what might happen the next morning when Marjorie wakes up and realizes not only that Bernice is gone but what she has done prior to leaving. Keeping in mind the character and motives of Marjorie, write a creative account of the aftermath the next morning detailing how Marjorie feels and how others react to her new hairstyle.

You may write from Marjorie's perspective or any perspective you wish, but make the story as detailed and as creative as possible. Craft a narrative that uses strong verbs and figurative language, much like Fitzgerald's story.

 Day 5: After You Read

Nonfiction Connection — Article

"Bernice Bobs Her Hair" was written in 1920, a time of social change and upheaval in America. The older women in the story, for example, consider bobbed hair to be an earmark of an immoral lifestyle, and Marjorie's worldview centers around the idea that the 20s are a new era and therefore require a new set of rules, scorning Bernice's old-fashioned ideas.

In the 1920s, the stern values of the previous two decades were slowly eroding in favor of a lighthearted America centered around having fun and living well. The glittering world of the 20s would soon succumb to Black Tuesday and the fall of the stock market, leading into the Great Depression; however, while this world lasted, it was a time of wonder and new ideals.

Locate **"1920s America: The Lowering of Morals and Raising of Hemlines" by Ciara Meehan.**

As you read,

- think about how Meehan describes the 1920s and how Fitzgerald describes the setting of "Bernice Bobs her Hair."
- make a list of the qualities of "flappers" as described by Meehan.

What are the similarities and differences between the "flappers" described in the article and the characters of Bernice and Marjorie in Fitzgerald's story?

In an organized paragraph, compare and contrast the flappers and the fictional young women, or discuss your answers with your teacher or fellow students.

Extended Activities

Essay – Based on the knowledge you have of 1920s America between "Bernice Bobs Her Hair" and Ciara Meehan's article, would you rather live in 1920s America or current America? Write a three-point expository essay on the subject and support your points with examples from the story, article, your own life, or additional research.

Dancing – Gather your friends and family and clear a large area. Using Youtube tutorials or other guides, learn the Charleston together and then choose some jazz or other 1920s music to accompany the dancing.

 Complete the Independent Practice on page 4 of the Resource Book.

 # Amigo Brothers

 Day 1: Before You Read

WHAT TO LEARN?
- Characters
- Making Predictions
- History
- Independent Practice

American Literature

Living for Tomorrow

High school students are pressured to earn good grades, participate in after-school activities, develop their talents and skills, and achieve athletic greatness. Many consider their future as dependent on their performance in these areas. Whether or not this is true, expectations for teenagers are extremely high.

Extracurricular activities, particularly sports, are especially important to low-income households and communities. Such programs can keep young adults from falling idle and turning to violent or criminal activity as well as encourage their self-confidence. Athletics can also provide opportunities for young adults to leave poor neighborhoods and move on to something better. If a teenager excels in athletics, they may go on to play collegiate or professional sports, which will bring them into a new walk of life, one very different from how they grew up.

Piri Thomas' short story "Amigo Brothers" describes the life of two young inner-city athletes who are both on the cusp of moving on to the next level in their sport of choice: boxing.

Meet the Author — Piri Thomas

Sep 30, 1928–Oct 17, 2011

Afro-Latino Heritage

The son of a Puerto Rican mother and a Cuban father, Thomas' writing (part of the Nuyorican Movement) deals with themes such as cultural identity and racial discrimination. His autobiography, *Down These Mean Streets*, describes his struggle growing up in the barrios of New York.

At-Risk Youth

Thomas' childhood in the NYC neighborhood of Spanish Harlem was rife with crime and violence. Children were expected to join gangs at a young age, and Thomas became involved with drugs and gang warfare. He spent seven years in prison for his choices. After he was released, he used his experiences to reach other at-risk youth and guide them down a different path.

FICTION 21

Day 2: Before You Read

Analyzing Literature — Characters

Categorizations of characters can be helpful when analyzing a work of fiction. One such categorization is dynamic or static. A **dynamic character** changes during the course of a story. Their emotions, actions, or mindsets undergo some kind of transformation because of the events of the narrative. In contrast, a static character does not change. A **static character** remains the same person at the end of the story as they were at the beginning. Readers can identify dynamic or static characters by comparing the characters at the beginning of the story with who they are at the end.

Additionally, characters can be flat or round. A **flat character** is uncomplicated, and the reader learns very little about them. Flat characters are sometimes used to simply move the plot along. A **round character**, on the other hand, is developed and complex. A reader gets to know round characters in depth. Someone can determine if characters are round or flat by placing them on a spectrum of development rather than putting them into a category.

J.R.R. Tolkien's fantasy novel *The Hobbit* contains dynamic and static as well as flat and round characters. The main character, Bilbo, undergoes an internal transformation during the story as he changes from fearful to courageous. In contrast, Gandalf (his mentor figure) remains the same throughout the narrative. Bilbo is dynamic, but Gandalf is static. Bilbo is also a round character, as is his adventure partner Thorin. The reader learns about these characters' pasts, what they value, and how they think. On the other hand, their comrades—such as Fili and Kili and Oin and Gloin—are not very developed; they are flat characters who simply move the plot forward.

Reading Focus: making predictions

Guessing what will happen next or **predicting** the outcome of a story can keep a reader engaged in the narrative. The work may meet a reader's expectations, but it may also surprise the reader with twists and turns.

My Prediction	Reasons for Prediction	Actual Outcome
"Amigo Brothers" will be about two Mexican brothers who are very close.	Amigo means "friend" in Spanish, and people from Mexico speak Spanish.	My prediction was wrong. The story was is about two Puerto Rican friends.

Reading Focus activity provided in the Resource Book on page 8.

Vocabulary

Many people belong to multilingual cultures. When authors write such characters, they may include some non-English words in the narration or dialogue to better reflect real life. Before reading "Amigo Brothers," find English equivalents for the Spanish words used in the story. (Some of the words are Puerto Rican slang.)

- amigo
- panin
- cheverote
- hermano
- sí
- suavecito
- sabe
- señores
- señoras
- Loisaida
- mucho corazón

Read "Amigo Brothers" by Piri Thomas

 Day 3: After You Read

Check Comprehension

1. **What** does the winner of the division finals get to do?

2. **Describe** Felix's fighting style and Antonio's fighting style.

3. **Who** wins the fight at the end of the story?

Think Critically

Sports are often seen as a way out of the hard life of the inner city. Thomas' short story mentions "street negatives," and Felix briefly encounters a gang. Winning the division finals and moving on to the championship could be Tony's or Felix's key to getting out of the inner city and achieving future success.

Think about how important winning this match is to both boys, the hard work they have put into their sport, and the opportunities they will have if they win. Also think about how important their friendship is to each other—how long they have known each other and how close they are. In this story, they have to choose which is more important: winning or friendship. Think about the inner turmoil that would result in this situation.

If you were in Tony's or Felix's position, how would you feel? Write an organized paragraph explaining your answer.

After you understand
what happens in a story and
why it happens, ask yourself,
what's the point?

Main Idea

"Amigo Brothers" begins by describing Antonio and Felix's close friendship. For most of the story, however, the two characters are either separated or fighting each other in the boxing ring. Antonio and Felix struggle throughout the narrative because they have to choose what is more valuable to them: their friendship or their boxing careers. The end of the story reveals their choice.

Consider the short story "Amigo Brothers" as a whole. What is the theme of the story? Write the theme in one complete sentence.

B

Consider how the story ends. In one complete sentence, explain why you think it was important to end the story this way.

FICTION 23

Analyzing Literature — Characters

Dynamic Character
A dynamic character changes during the course of a story. Their emotions, actions, or mindsets undergo some kind of transformation.

Static Character
A static character does not change. They remain the same person at the end of the story as they were at the beginning.

Flat Character
A flat character is uncomplicated, and the reader learns very little about them. They are sometimes used to simply move the plot along.

Round Character
A round character is developed and complex. A reader gets to know them, their past, thoughts, and feelings in depth.

Changes in a character can be more developed in longer works like novels; however, characters in short stories can be dynamic as well. Antonio and Felix in "Amigo Brothers" undergo changes of heart and mind. Analyzing the story can reveal how they think and feel in the beginning, what causes them to change, and how they finish the narrative.

"Amigo Brothers" also contains both flat and round characters. When judging a character's flatness or roundness, it is better to determine where they fall on a flat-round spectrum rather than simply stating if they are flat or round.

Identify how Antonio's and Felix's views about their friendship and boxing change throughout the narrative. Also, determine where characters fall on a flat-round spectrum.

Antonio and Felix		
At the beginning of the story, Antonio and Felix value….	The friends are forced to change because…	At the end of the story, Antonio and Felix value…

[*Character*] Flat ●————— Round

Analyzing Literature activity provided in the Resource Book on page 10.

DIVE DEEPER

1. **Apply** – Identify the climax of "Amigo Brothers" and explain your choice.

2. **Analyze** – After the final bell dings and the match is over, Tony and Felix rush at each other. Contrast the crowd's expectation with the reality of what happens.

3. **Evaluate** – Explain how the *setting* affects the conflict in "Amigo Brothers."

 **Day 4: After You Read**

Analyzing Literature

Internal conflict is a struggle within a character, otherwise known as person vs. self. When a character undergoes internal conflict, they struggle with their own thoughts or emotions.

1. What *internal conflict* do Antonio and Felix experience during the story? Identify what forces are struggling in their hearts and minds.

2. Which conflict is greater in "Amigo Brothers"—the *internal conflict* or the *external conflict*? Explain your answer.

Connection Reflection

3. At the beginning of the story, Tony and Felix discuss the coming boxing match in which they will be pitted against each other. They decide to stay away from each other until after the fight. Do you think this was a good decision? Why or why not?

4. Even though both boys want to mentally prepare for the fight, Tony and Felix spend the night before in different ways. Because of how they spend their final night, they each come up with different mindsets about the next day. Compare and contrast Felix's and Tony's attitudes going into the fight.

Writing Connection

The expression "caught between a rock and a hard place" means that someone must make a choice between two equally unpleasant things. For example, someone may have to choose between putting their aging dog to sleep or letting the dog live in pain. Neither choice is appealing.

In Piri Thomas' story, Antonio and Felix have to choose between two difficult options. On the one hand, they could lose the match, but they do not want to lose. On the other hand, in order to win, they must injure their best friend. This is equally disagreeable.

Have you ever been in a situation where you were caught between a rock and a hard place? Write a personal journal entry about the situation, the outcome, and how you felt. Date the entry. Because this is a personal journal entry, you can be explicitly honest; no one else needs to read your journal.

FICTION 25

 Day 5: After You Read

Nonfiction Connection — History

The boxing match in Piri Thomas' "Amigo Brothers" is an elimination match to decide who would represent the Boys Club in the citywide Golden Gloves Championship Tournament. Golden Gloves tournaments are annual competitions in amateur boxing. This match was extremely important to Antonio and Felix.

Like many sports, boxing has an interesting history (one going back thousands of years), and boxing has influenced culture in surprising ways. For example, an ancient Roman statue displays the fatigue of a resting boxer. In the twenty-first century, a popular internet meme (the "Overly Manly Man") pictures the bare-knuckled American boxer Mike Conley (b. 1860).

One of the most notable moments in boxing history coincided with a very important moment in Western Civilization. In the year 1938—before World War II began but within the reign of Adolf Hitler, an avid white supremacist—the African-American boxer Joe Louis stepped into the ring against German champion Max Schmeling. Schmeling was not a Nazi (he even had a Jewish manager), but the public viewed the fight as an important ideological clash between Germany and the United States.

Look up **"The Fight of the Century: Louis vs. Schmeling" by NPR** to find out the results of the match. Also, listen to the original radio broadcast of the match, **The Joe Louis-Max Schemling Boxing Match, Broadcast June 22, 1938,** found on the same page.

As you read and listen,
- note the energy of the crowd and the excitement of the announcer
- identify how many people were invested in this match—in both America and Germany

Why was this fight so important to so many people? Why does this boxing match deserve the title "The Fight of the Century"? Write an organized paragraph explaining your answers or discuss your answers with your teacher or fellow students.

Extended Activities

1) **Sports** – Attend a local boxing match or sporting event. Compare the experience to how the story described the local boxing match between Antonio and Felix in the Lower East Side.

2) **Interview** – Interview an athlete about their experience in their sport. The athlete can be a professional, retired, or an amateur. Prepare interview questions and set up a time and place to meet.

 Complete the Independent Practice on page 12 of the Resource Book.

The Necklace

Day 1: Before You Read

WHAT TO LEARN?
- Conflict
- Visualize
- Encyclopedia Entry
- Independent Practice

I'll be happy *if*...

"If only my parents were rich..."
   "I can't wait until I get out of high school."
"Once I get into college, everything will work out."
   "If I could only afford my own car..."
"When I get my own place, I'll be happy."
   "Once summer comes, I'll be happy."
"When I get in a relationship, I'll be happy."
   "Once I start making money, I'll be happy."

Some people think they can only be happy if something were different, if their life changes, or if they get something they do not have. Once their situation changes, however, or if they receive what they desired, they may find that they are still dissatisfied. There will always be something more—something else that promises happiness.

Many people live their lives with such discontentment, never appreciating that which they do have. Have you ever wanted something that, in the end, was not all that you thought it would be? "The Necklace" by Guy de Maupassant tells such a tale, focusing on a dissatisfied woman named Mathilde.

World Literature

Meet the Author — Guy de Maupassant

Aug 5, 1850–July 6, 1893

Realism

Minor dramas and little preoccupations fill the lives of ordinary people, and Maupassant included these details in his writing. In an attempt to present life as it really is, Maupassant avoided all traces of romantic idealism—that is, portraying life in a grand and fantastical way. His stories, rather, fit into the literary category of realism.

No Judgment

In his short stories and novels, Maupassant included characters ranging from the lower class to the upper class of French society. He described the people indifferently, neither condemning their faults nor praising their strengths. For example, in "The Necklace," readers encounter the characters without a narrator telling them what to think.

FICTION 27

Analyzing Literature: Conflict

Day 2: Before You Read

Conflict is the struggle between opposing forces. In literature, conflict is intertwined with plot. Characters involved in a story seek to either resolve or avoid the conflict, and their actions in doing so propel the plot forward. Literature contains two major categories of conflict: *external conflict* and *internal conflict*, which can be subdivided even further.

External Conflict	
Person vs. Person	Person vs. Nature
Person vs. Society	

In *person vs. person*, a character struggles against another human being, like a thief, an enemy soldier, or a sibling. In *person vs. nature*, a character struggles against some kind of natural phenomenon, like a storm, a dense forest, or animals. In *person vs. society*, a character struggles with an intangible element of their culture, such as poverty, racism, or unfair laws.

Internal Conflict
Person vs. Self

In *person vs. self*, a character struggles with their own thoughts or emotions. For example, in Jane Austen's novel *Pride and Prejudice*, the main character Elizabeth has both external and internal struggles. She clashes with snooty members of high society but eventually realizes that she acts just like them, making judgments based on pride and vain prejudice. She experiences internal conflict between who she wants to be and who she actually is. One of the most famous lines from the books is, "Till this moment, I never knew myself." After this internal struggle, Elizabeth must decide how to act from then on.

Reading Focus: visualize

Authors often include imagery in their writing–that is, detailed language that appeals to a reader's senses. **Visualizing** these details is one way to connect with what you are reading.

The Ministry Ball	The 10 Years of Poverty

Reading Focus activity provided in the Resource Book on page 16.

Vocabulary

"The Necklace" was originally written in French. When translating works from other languages, scholars have to choose between multiple synonyms that could stand for the original foreign word. Find at least two synonyms for each of the vocabulary words listed.

delicacy
wit
gallantries
inscrutable
triumph
ecstasy
rapturously
gracious
ruinous
heroically
odious

Read "The Necklace" by Guy de Maupassant

 Day 3: After You Read

Check Comprehension

1. *What* is the name of Mathilde's rich friend and former schoolmate?

2. *Describe* the Loisels' plan to pay off the thirty-six thousand francs.

3. *What* is the surprise ending?

Think Critically

Maupassant's twist ending may have inspired a similar tale across the Atlantic. In the United States, O'Henry wrote "The Gift of the Magi" in which a poor husband and wife each sacrifice precious things in order to buy their spouse a Christmas gift. The sacrifices they make, however, render each other's gifts useless. Even so, they are happy to be together. (If you are unfamiliar with the O'Henry story, reading a summary may assist you in completing this activity.)

Why does the end of "The Gift of the Magi" have an uplifting feeling but the end of "The Necklace" have a depressing feeling? What is different about the endings?

Write an organized paragraph explaining your answer.

After you understand **what** happens in a story and **why** it happens, ask yourself, **what's the point?**

Main Idea

Mathilde is dissatisfied with her middle class life. She wants more money, finer clothes, a fancier house, and a higher social status. She is given the chance to experience this "upper class life" for one night, and she borrows the titular necklace to do so. When she loses this necklace, she spends the next ten years of her life very poor as she attempts to pay back the 36,000 francs the replacement necklace cost.

Considering that the original necklace turned out to be a fake, what insight about life might the reader gain from reading this story? You may want to consider what the fake necklace symbolizes. In one complete sentence, describe the main point of the story.

Consider what Mathilde desired at the beginning of the story, what she did to achieve these desires, and what actually became of her in the end. With this in mind, what lesson can you gain from the story and apply to yourself personally? In one complete sentence, explain how the story can relate to your own life.

FICTION

Analyzing Literature — Conflict

Conflict is the struggle between opposing forces. There are two major categories of conflict: *external conflict* and *internal conflict.*

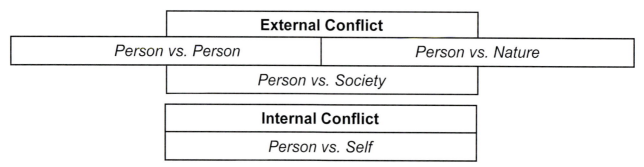

In **person vs. person,** a character struggles against another human being. In **person vs. nature,** a character struggles against some natural phenomenon. In **person vs. society,** a character struggles with an intangible element of their culture. In **person vs. self,** a character struggles with their own thoughts or emotions.

In literature, external and internal conflict may overlap in the same story. This is the case in Maupassant's "The Necklace," which contains examples of both external and internal conflict.

Find examples of both internal and external conflict in "The Necklace." Identify the type of conflict present, record the opposing forces, and then explain the nature of the conflict.

Internal Conflict		
Type of Conflict	**Opposing forces**	**Nature of the Conflict**
Person vs. Self	Mr. Loisel vs. how to spend his money	Mr. Loisel wants to spend 400 francs to go on a hunting trip, but his wife says she needs the money for a new dress.

Analyzing Literature activity provided in the Resource Book on page 18.

DIVE DEEPER

1. **Apply** – Identify what causes Mathilde to borrow the necklace in the first place.

2. **Analyze** – A *static* character does not change during a story, but a *dynamic* character does. Classify Mathilde as a static or a dynamic character. Explain your answer.

3. **Evaluate** – Compare how Mathilde is described at the beginning of the story and at the end of the story. How does her physical appearance change from the beginning of the story and the end?

▶ Day 4: After You Read

Analyzing Literature

Irony is a contrast or inconsistency between expectations and reality. Something in literature is ironic when what occurs is different than what the reader or the characters expected.

1. How does the end of "The Necklace" demonstrate irony?

2. How would the theme of the story have been different without the ironic twist?

Connection Reflection

3. The reader witnesses all the hardships that befall Mathilde and her husband following her loss of the necklace. After reading about all their toils, the reader learns the truth at the same time Mathilde does. Do you feel sorry for Mathilde at the end of the story? Why or why not?

4. Reread the scene when Mathilde arrives home and looks at herself in the mirror, having just experienced her perfect night. If she had not lost the necklace, do you think Mathilde would have been happy, now that she has experienced what she has always wanted? Explain your answer.

Writing Connection

Mathilde suffered ceaselessly, feeling herself born to enjoy all delicacies and all luxuries. She was distressed at the poverty of her dwelling, at the bareness of the walls, at the shabby chairs, the ugliness of the curtains. All those things, of which another woman of her rank would never even have been conscious, tortured her and made her angry....She thought of long reception halls hung with ancient silk, of the dainty cabinets containing priceless curiosities and of the little coquettish perfumed reception rooms made for chatting at five o'clock with intimate friends, with men famous and sought after, whom all women envy and whose attention they all desire.

Imagine that you are Mathilde's friend. She has sent you a letter complaining about how she is dissatisfied with her life, expressing thoughts and feelings similar to those in this excerpt from the story.

Write a response letter to Mathilde. Think about how you would counsel her about her predicament. Think about how you believe she should respond to her situation and what you think she needs to hear.

Properly format the composition as a letter should be formatted.

 Day 5: After You Read

Nonfiction Connection — Encyclopedia Entry

Scholars divide literary history into movements and time periods, such as Renaissance literature, romanticism, modernism, and many others. Guy de Maupassant's writing fits into a category of literature called realism. Other realist writers include Mark Twain and Jack London in the United States, George Eliot (aka Mary Anne Evans) in the United Kingdom, and Anton Chekov in Russia.

What is literary realism?

To answer such a question, someone may consult an encyclopedia, either from the library or on the internet. Encyclopedia entries contain general information on various topics, and such entries do not include as many specifics as, for example, a literature textbook. However, an encyclopedia entry is more approachable for someone unfamiliar with a specific area of study.

Look up the following entry on the *Literary Devices* website: **Examples and Definition of Realism**

Read the entire entry. As you read,
- identify what each example illustrates about the characteristics of realism, even if you are not familiar with the example literary works
- locate a sentence or phrase that can function as a concise definition of realism

How are the characteristics of realism, as described in the entry, reflected in Guy de Maupassant's "The Necklace"? In other words, why do scholars claim Maupassant's short story is an example of realist literature?

Write an organized paragraph explaining your answer or discuss your answer with your teacher or fellow students.

Extended Activities

Music – "The Necklace" mentioned Mathilde's dancing to music at the Ministry Ball. Research the kind of music that was popular in France in the late 1800s. Find and listen to recordings of music from that era.

Manual Labor – Part of Mathilde's fall into poverty resulted in her knowing "what heavy housework meant." In order to experience the kind of physical labor that Mathilde experienced, offer your services to a friend or family member to perform hard labor. Offer to mow the lawn, to sweep and mop the floors, to wash the windows, or something similar.

 Complete the Independent Practice on page 20 of the Resource Book.

Harrison Bergeron

Day 1: Before You Read

WHAT TO LEARN?

- Theme
- Compare and Contrast
- Birography
- Independent Practice

Some are more *equal* than others...

If you spend any amount of time with younger children, you will likely hear "It's not fair!" before too long—perhaps someone got a bigger cookie or a longer timeout. Children are not the only ones who are obsessed with fairness, however; humanity is born with the innate desire to have an equal share of life and everything in it. Social and political movements have begun with the premise of equality for all. Some, such as the Civil Rights movement, made a great impact; others, such as socialism and communism, were not so successful.

Most would agree that the idea of equality is inherently good. The Declaration of Independence states that "all men are created equal," but is this true? Does every person possess the same skills, talents, and qualities? Furthermore, can there be such a thing as too much equality? Should people be exactly the same in all measures to enforce total equality? Discuss your answers with your teacher or fellow students.

American Literature

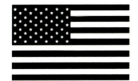

Meet the Author — Kurt Vonnegut

So It Goes...

Vonnegut's novels and short stories can loosely be classified under both science fiction and satire. The people and places may be outlandish, but the events and humanity of his characters are distinctly familiar. "All this happened, more or less," he begins one novel, and the same applies to his other works.

Art Imitates Life

Vonnegut not only served in the United States Army during WWII but was captured by Germany and imprisoned in an underground meat locker called Schlachthof-Funf, or Slaughterhouse-Five, a name he later used for his most popular novel. As a result of his experiences during the war, much of his writing satirizes war, the government, and their effects on society.

Nov 11, 1922–Apr 11, 2007

FICTION **33**

Day 2: Before You Read

Analyzing Literature — Theme

Contrary to popular understanding, *theme* in literature cannot be fully described in one or two words; instead, the theme is a pervasive meaning woven throughout the story and expressed as a full sentence. A word such as "freedom" describes an element of a story but is not a theme; a sentence such as "the government should not interfere with the freedom of its citizens" can be a theme, for it describes the significance of the story rather than just one element of the story. This is a possible theme for the novel *Nineteen Eighty-Four* by George Orwell, for in this novel, the government controls not only its citizens' actions but also their thoughts. Orwell might not offer such a theme so explicitly, but the novel demonstrates this theme through its negative portrayal of the government and its sympathetic view of the citizens.

Some authors prefer to make their themes evident to the reader while others prefer a more subtle approach. Themes can be lessons or instructions to the reader, or they may simply be an observation of humanity.

Reading Focus: compare and contrast

"Harrison Bergeron" is a *dystopia*, an imagined society that, unlike utopias, is not perfect or pleasant but is hopeless and generally controlled by a totalitarian government. Dystopias are often written as critiques of the author's society. They parallel elements of that society to show that, while a dystopia may seem far-fetched, it is not as impossible as one might imagine.

Similarities with Your Society	Differences with Your Society
Everyone wants to be equal with everyone else.	People aren't forced to be equal to others.

Reading Focus activity provided in the Resource Book on page 24.

Vocabulary

Most words carry with them a certain tone. Just as connotations give words shades of meaning, tone gives words shades of feeling. As you read "Harrison Bergeron," consider the words Vonnegut chose to use for the story. Do they give the story a certain tone? If so, what is the tone? When you find each word in the right column in the story, look up its definition and use it in a sentence similar to those written by Vonnegut.

sashweight
birdshot
impediment
grackle
consternation
caper
gambol

Read "Harrison Bergeron" by Kurt Vonnegut

 Day 3: After You Read

Check Comprehension

1. *How* old is Harrison Bergeron?

2. *Who* is Diana Moon Glampers?

3. *What* happens to Harrison Bergeron at the end of the story?

Think Critically

"Harrison Bergeron" is a satirical short story, and satire is generally written as social critique and commentary. Jonathan Swift's satiric "A Modest Proposal," for example, was written in 1729 during Ireland's food shortage. It suggested that starving citizens eat their babies as a response to the government's outlandish ideas of how to solve Ireland's crisis. He was not serious, of course, but instead wanted to show the government how ridiculous their solutions were.

What might the author Kurt Vonnegut be criticizing through the story "Harrison Bergeron"? Is his critique justified? Write an organized paragraph that explains your answers to these questions.

After you understand
what happens in a story and
why it happens, ask yourself,
what's the point?

Main Idea

In "Harrison Bergeron," everyone is forced to be equal even though not all people are equal in intelligence, physical capability, beauty, and other factors. Those who are stronger, more intelligent, and more beautiful must handicap or disguise themselves in order to be equal to those around them.

Toward the end of the story, Harrison tries to overthrow the system but is literally shot down. What is the purpose of showing such a society and recounting a failed attempt to change it? Summarize the main idea in one complete sentence.

This story was written in 1961 and is set in 2081, similar to other dystopian works such as 1984 and Brave New World that predicted societies in the future. Could such a society as the one in "Harrison Bergeron" exist in 2081 or sooner? In one complete sentence, describe in your own words why such a society is or is not possible in real life.

FICTION

Analyzing Literature — Theme

The *theme* of a story is the meaning a story has or the significance of a story. Depending on the literature itself, theme may be fairly easy or fairly difficult to decipher. Some authors prefer subtle themes while other authors prefer to state a story's theme blatantly. The tools below can help you discern a story's theme if it is not obvious.

- Close Reading: Can you decipher any deeper or double meanings in the story? Do setting, character names, or events have significance beyond their surface value?
- Repetition: Important elements of a story that lead to its theme may be emphasized and repeated. When authors use repetition, they are generally signifying something important.
- The Good and the Bad: What in the story is portrayed as good? What is portrayed as bad? The story's dichotomy of good and evil may help you discover the theme.

In a complete sentence, explain your interpretation of the theme of "Harrison Bergeron." Then, support your explanation of the theme in an organized paragraph that uses details from the story.

THEME

Write the theme here

SUPPORTING PARAGRAPH

The theme I chose is correct because...(include three reasons)

Analyzing Literature activity provided in the Resource Book on page 26.

DIVE DEEPER

1. **Apply** – The society in "Harrison Bergeron" is a dystopia because it attempts to make everyone equal even though people have different strengths and weaknesses. Develop an improved society that does not require total equality but instead recognizes the differences between people. Why is your society superior?

2. **Analyze** – In the story, the most handsome man (Harrison) and the most beautiful woman (the ballerina) aspire to be the leaders of society and are killed because they refuse to be equal to everyone else. Compare their attempt to rule with those who try to gain power in your society. What are the similarities and differences?

3. **Evaluate** – *Mood* is the feelings a reader experiences during a story. Assess the mood of "Harrison Bergeron." How does it contribute to or affect the theme of the story? How would a different mood produce a different story?

Day 4: After You Read

Analyzing Literature

In literature, **satire** is a form of writing that uses humor, exaggeration, sarcasm, or ridicule in order to expose or critique a person, a people group, an aspect of society, or society itself. Satire has existed as a form of critique since Greek and Roman literature and is usually written to shame a group or individual or to make readers aware of an important situation. Though satire often uses humor, it is not a required aspect; indeed, satire is often a serious subject.

1. What does "Harrison Bergeron" use in order to make its critique—humor, exaggeration, sarcasm, or ridicule? You may choose more than one method. Explain your answer with supporting details from the story.

2. Satire is most effective when the concept it is critiquing is a current topic or event. "Harrison Bergeron" was written in 1961; is it still relevant in your society? Why or why not?

Connection Reflection

3. *"A twenty-one-gun salute in his head stopped that...It was such a doozy that George was white and trembling, and tears stood on the rims of his red eyes."*
In "Harrison Bergeron," those who are mentally or physically more proficient than the average citizen must endure handicaps in order to make them equal to those who are average. Do these handicaps have any parallel in your society? If so, what are they? If not, do you think they might ever be implemented? Explain your answer.

4. *"Forget sad things," said George. "I always do," said Hazel.*
Making everyone equal should make everyone happy; at least, this might be a maxim of the government in "Harrison Bergeron." However, is everyone in such a society happy? Support your answer with details from the text.

Writing Connection

Imagine that you work for the newspaper in Harrison Bergeron's society and have just been assigned to write a short newspaper article describing the death of Harrison Bergeron and the ballerina, his supposed empress, as well as his attempt to take control of society and give it freedom. Write as though you are a member of Harrison's society who condemns what Harrison tried to do. Research the structure of newspaper articles to make your article as realistic as possible.

 Day 5: After You Read

Nonfiction Connection — Biography

"Harrison Bergeron" is a relatively tame yet typical example of Kurt Vonnegut's work: fiction that makes use of the outlandish to prove a point about society. His works are highly *postmodern*, meaning they disagree with absolutes of theories and ideologies and do not necessarily conform to an agreed standard of art.

Vonnegut is often described as a *humanist*, or someone who attributes more importance to humanity than to higher powers or deities. His works reflect this belief and, as a result, have garnered criticism from readers and reviewers who do not subscribe to humanism and therefore view his works as fatalist and heretical. His most famous work, *Slaughterhouse-Five*, has been banned numerous times from libraries, and copies have even been burned in protest.

Locate **"Kurt Vonnegut: American Novelist," a biography published by Encyclopedia Britannica online.**

- consider how Vonnegut's experiences, especially those in WWII, shaped his worldview of humanism and thus shaped his fiction.
- decide whether or not the subject matter of his works warrants censorship, banning, or burning.

After reading about Vonnegut's life and his ideology, do you think his books would have had equal impact on society if they were not so offensive? Why or why not? In an organized paragraph, write your response and support it with three points, or discuss your answer with your teacher or fellow students.

Extended Activities

Current Literature – Dystopian literature has peaked since the turn of the century, becoming popular in not only general fiction but also young adult fiction as well. Find at least two other dystopias written in the twenty-first century and compare them to "Harrison Bergeron." Do they include any of the same elements, ideas, or critiques? Why has the popularity of dystopian literature increased recently? Discuss your answers with your teacher or fellow students.

Discussion – With friends or family members, decide how each individual would need to be handicapped in order to make the group's members equal to one another. What kind of handicaps are needed to balance each person's strengths? If possible, implement the handicaps (but avoid loud noises directly in someone's ears) and discuss the results.

 Complete the Independent Practice on page 28 of the Resource Book.

The Yellow Wallpaper

Day 1: Before You Read

WHAT TO LEARN?

- **Irony**
- Drawing Conclusions
- Article
- Independent Practice

American Literature

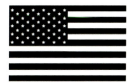

When people don't UNDERSTAND

Problems and feelings can be difficult to express. When someone cannot properly express how they feel, that person may think they are unable to ask for help. This can lead to believing that they are alone, even if they are surrounded by other people.

When a person does ask for help, sometimes other people simply do not understand. They might discredit one's problems or feelings, saying they are not serious or even real. Other times, they might offer bad advice to deal with the issues. This can lead to a feeling of hopelessness in the one who is suffering.

Dealing with internal problems is not hopeless, however, and people who struggle are not alone. Finding the proper help and not giving up is key. When a person isolates themselves, for one reason or another, the problems can increase. "The Yellow Wallpaper" by Charlotte Perkins Gilman is a story of someone who is given bad advice, isolates herself, and suffers for it.

Meet the Author — Charlotte Perkins Gilman

Social Reformer

Through her lifestyle and her writing, Gilman sought to change the way women were viewed and treated in her time. She argued against locking women into only "domestic roles"—meaning their sole purpose in life is to cook, clean, and raise children, with nothing concerning professional, intellectual, or creative pursuits.

A Struggle with Depression

As she was already susceptible to depression, living a sheltered married life and suffering from serious postpartum depression after giving birth pushed Gilman's sanity to the breaking point. "The Yellow Wallpaper" is a fictional account of Gilman's experience battling mental illness, which was mistreated by the doctors of her time. Although she did recover, Gilman writes that she was never truly the same.

July 3, 1860–Aug 17, 1935

FICTION

Day 2: Before You Read

Analyzing Literature — Irony

In literature, *irony* is a contrast or inconsistency between expectations and reality. Irony can be divided into three main categories:

- *Verbal Irony*—when something a character says is different than what the character means
- *Situational Irony*—when the outcome of a situation is different than what was expected
- *Dramatic Irony*—when the audience knows something the characters in a story do not know

Dramatic irony often results in either humor or powerful suspense. Characters in a story are not always aware of the thoughts and actions of other characters, but the reader is aware of them. This can happen when the author writes a scene that does not contain some of the characters or when the author provides insight into a character's inner thoughts. Dramatic irony occurs when the characters in a story make decisions based on their limited knowledge, but only the reader understands if these decisions are right or wrong.

For example, at the end of Shakespeare's play about the unfortunate lovers *Romeo and Juliet,* the audience knows that Juliet is faking her death so that she can run away and be with Romeo. Unfortunately, Romeo does not have this knowledge. Romeo kills himself to be united with Juliet in death, thus frustrating the audience and demonstrating dramatic irony.

Reading Focus: drawing conclusions

In fiction, not everything is explicitly stated. To create suspense or mystery, authors may include only hints for the reader to piece together. Combining these hints with one's knowledge of reality or the rest of the story is **drawing conclusions** about things that are not clearly revealed in the text.

Details from the Story	My Knowledge	My Conclusion
"John laughs at me, of course, but one expects that in marriage."	People laugh at others when they think they are foolish.	John thinks his wife is foolish, and the narrator thinks this is normal.

Reading Focus activity provided in the Resource Book on page 32.

Vocabulary

Familiarize yourself with the words listed on the right before reading "The Yellow Wallpaper." Use a dictionary to find their definitions. As you read "The Yellow Wallpaper," look for these words and pay attention to how the narrator uses them. Would you use such words in your personal journal?

felicity
lurid
draught
atrocious
conspicuous
querulous
undulating
arabesque
conscientiously

Read "The Yellow Wallpaper" by Charlotte Perkins Gilman

 Day 3: After You Read

Check Comprehension

1. **What** is happening to the narrator as the story goes on?

2. **What** does the narrator think she sees behind the yellow wallpaper and out in the open country?

3. **Why** does the narrator tear at the wallpaper at the end of the story?

Think Critically

Scholars often compare the horror of Charlotte Perkins Gilman's "The Yellow Wallpaper" with the horror of Edgar Allan Poe's writings, such as "The Raven," "The Masque of the Red Death," and "The Cask of Amontillado." These Poe stories were intended to excite terror within the reader.

Based on your reading of "The Yellow Wallpaper" and your knowledge of Gilman's history, do you think this story is primarily meant to disturb readers? If not, does the story have another purpose? If so, what do you think the purpose is?

Write an organized paragraph explaining your answer.

After you understand **what** happens in a story and **why** it happens, ask yourself, **what's the point?**

Main Idea

"The Yellow Wallpaper" is a fictional story based on Charlotte Gilman's real life experience. The narrator of "The Yellow Wallpaper"—like many women in the author's time period—is instructed by multiple doctors to seclude herself and be inactive in order to remedy her "nervous depression."

Considering what happens to the narrator when she follows this prescription, what do you think is the main idea of "The Yellow Wallpaper," the most important point made by the story? In one complete sentence, describe what you think is the main point of this story.

Considering that this story was written in the late 1800s and reflects how women were treated at that time, think about whether or not this story can apply to modern readers. In one complete sentence, describe why "The Yellow Wallpaper" does or does not have something to offer to modern readers.

FICTION

Analyzing Literature — Irony

In literature, ***irony*** is a contrast or inconsistency between expectations and reality. ***Dramatic irony*** is when the audience knows something the characters in a story do not know. Characters in a story are not always aware of the thoughts and actions of other characters, but the reader is aware of them. Dramatic irony occurs when characters make decisions based on their limited knowledge, but only the reader understands if these decisions are right or wrong.

The dramatic irony in "The Yellow Wallpaper" occurs primarily because the narrator does not realize she is losing her mind, but the reader slowly comes to this understanding. Even as the story is filtered through the narrator's unbalanced mind, the reader understands that how the narrator describes things is not necessarily how they truly are. Also, sometimes the other characters believe one thing, but the opposite is true.

Identify points in "The Yellow Wallpaper" that demonstrate dramatic irony. Record how the narrator explains a situation and what the true explanation is.

What is the situation?	How does this demonstrate dramatic irony?
John believes that letting the narrator spend most of her time resting in the room with yellow wallpaper is helping the narrator recover.	*Being in the room with yellow wallpaper is not helping the narrator recover; it is, in fact, worsening her condition.*

Analyzing Literature activity provided in the Resource Book on page 34.

DIVE DEEPER

1. **Apply** – *Symbolism* is when something in a story represents something else. If you were to choose something from the story that acted as a symbol, what would you choose? Explain your answer.

2. **Analyze** – Does the yellow wallpaper cause the narrator's madness, or is her reaction to the paper an effect of her madness? Support your answer.

3. **Evaluate** – *Conflict* can be *external* (between one character and another) or *internal* (between a character and their own mind). Determine which is greater in this story: the internal or external conflict. How do you know?

Day 4: After You Read

Analyzing Literature

The view from which a story is told is called its **point of view**. When a story is told in **first-person** point of view, the reader must understand that the information they are given is filtered through the narrator's mind.

1. In "The Yellow Wallpaper," is the first-person narrator **reliable**? That is, is the information presented through the narrator always accurate? Why or why not?

2. How would this story have been different if it were told in **third-person** point of view? Support your answer with specific examples.

Connection Reflection

3. The narrator of "The Yellow Wallpaper" was told to seclude herself and be inactive to help her condition. Unfortunately, this advice only worsened her problems. What do you think would have actually helped her?

4. The narrator writes that she tried to explain to others that there was something wrong with her. John, however, "does not believe [she] is sick!" Suppose a friend or family member came to you and shared that they feel like something is wrong, even though they appear healthy. How would you respond?

Writing Connection

"The Yellow Wallpaper" is written as a series of journal entries from the narrator. Because of this, most of the story is spent describing the inner workings of the narrator's mind—what she feels, thinks, and imagines. Occasionally, she describes some action or a conversation she had with another character.

If her husband John kept a similar kind of journal, what would his entries look like? Write one journal entry (or more, if you choose) from John's perspective that takes place at the same time as the entries of "The Yellow Wallpaper." Consider what is going on in John's mind, what he sees, and how he would explain his wife's behavior.

Try to include the same things that the narrator of "The Yellow Wallpaper" included in her journal entries. Record actions John witnesses, conversations he has or overhears, and something that is occupying his mind.

 Day 5: After You Read

Nonfiction Connection — Article

Gilman's short story "The Yellow Wallpaper" describes doctors who misunderstand mental health issues. The narrator's husband John insists that the narrator does not have a real problem because she is physically healthy. He will not listen to her arguments otherwise, but the end of the story clearly shows that John was wrong.

Mindsets about mental health have changed significantly since the publication of "The Yellow Wallpaper" in the 1890s. People who struggle with internal problems, such as anxiety and depression, are taken much more seriously than they have been in the past. Anxiety and depression are different than the hysteria and mild schizophrenia displayed by the narrator of "The Yellow Wallpaper"; however, both are valid mental health issues that need to be addressed.

Look up **Mental Health America's online article "Depression in Teens."**

As you read,
- create a list of possible symptoms of depression in teens.
- create a list of how the article encourages people to avoid depression as well as how to deal with already onset depression.

After you read, compare the lists you created from the article with the story "The Yellow Wallpaper." What similarities or differences are there between the narrator's behavior and the symptoms of depression? How does the advice of the doctors in "The Yellow Wallpaper" differ from the advice in the Mental Health America article?

Write an organized paragraph explaining your answers or discuss your answers with your teacher or fellow students.

Extended Activities

Research – Research how mental health has been viewed in the past as well as how it is viewed now. Use the internet or books to find information and record your findings on a sheet of paper.

Art – The narrator of "The Yellow Wallpaper" spends a majority of the story describing the strange pattern on the walls of her bedroom. Based on the narrator's descriptions, create a design for the wallpaper. An exact replica of what the narrator describes may not be possible, for the narrator's descriptions are often tainted with insanity, but do your best to create a design for the yellow wallpaper.

 Complete the Independent Practice on page 36 of the Resource Book.

The Speckled Band

📖 Day 1: Before You Read

WHAT TO LEARN?
- Mood
- Making Predictions
- Review
- Independent Practice

Something wicked *this way comes...*

Have you ever encountered a situation that unnerved or frightened you? Perhaps it was caused by someone else, or perhaps you did not know the cause, which made the situation worse. While humanity has discovered much about the world, much of it still remains a mystery, and this mystery—in the wrong time and place—can alarm us.

In situations like these, we can often find a logical explanation for mysterious events, as you will observe in the adventure of Sherlock Holmes and Dr. Watson. Thinking rationally, even when you face something unknown or terrifying, can provide a solution that explains what was previously a mystery. Assuming that the lights in an old house are flickering because of an electrical problem, not because of something supernatural, is a rational response to an unnerving situation. Replacing the lightbulbs or checking the breaker box could solve the mystery completely.

If you have encountered such a situation, how did you react? Were you calm or uneasy? Do you wish you had reacted differently? Discuss your answers with your teacher or fellow classmates.

British Literature

Meet the Author — Sir Arthur Conan Doyle

The Good Doctor

Prior to his knighting, Doyle was educated as a physician and practiced medicine while writing fiction. His knowledge of the medical field gave credibility to Dr. John Watson, the wounded war medic who assists Sherlock Holmes.

"I Think of Slaying Holmes"

Although Sherlock Holmes has been adored since his inception, Doyle was famously ambivalent toward the detective, often wishing to kill him off so Doyle could focus on other literary pursuits. He charged exorbitant prices for Sherlock stories, hoping to dissuade publication, but publishers eagerly paid the high prices, making Doyle one of the best-paid authors of all time.

May 22, 1859–July 7, 1930

FICTION

Day 2: Before You Read

Analyzing Literature — Mood

Just like humans can portray a particular mood, a story has an emotional *mood*. If a person is frowning or talking angrily, their mood is easy to discern. In the same way, if a book presents its content negatively, that is a clue toward its mood.

Sometimes referred to as the atmosphere of a story, mood evokes a certain feeling from the reader that aids in understanding the story. Do you feel encouraged? Depressed? Suspicious? Your reaction is a good barometer of mood.

While your reaction is helpful, the author provides clues to help you discern the mood as well. Where or in what time does the story take place? What is the main point of the story? How do characters speak to each other or about the story's events? Asking these and similar questions can guide you to the story's mood.

Setting, theme, and **diction** are important indicators of mood.

Reading Focus: making predictions

Making predictions while reading a story keeps you engaged and invested in the characters and the plot. In detective stories, trying to find the solution before the detective does can be thrilling—especially if you are correct—but it is also a good exercise in logical thinking.

Event from "The Speckled Band"	My Prediction	What Happened?
Miss Stoner tells Sherlock that her fiancé does not believe her story.	*Miss Stoner's fiancé underestimates her experiences.*	*I was correct—he writes off her worries as trivial, unrelated things.*

Reading Focus activity provided in the Resource Book on page 40.

Vocabulary

"The Speckled Band" is a British story written in the nineteenth century, which results in two cautions for vocabulary: archaic words may be used, and words may be spelled or used differently. As you read the story, watch for "odd," "draught," and "dummy." In the story's geographical and historical context, these words mean something different than their initial appearance suggests. Also, other words, such as "fain" and "fortnight," are rarely used in contemporary English.

odd
haggard
dissolute
morose
parapet
fortnight
fain
averse
gaiters
pittance
draught
stile
dummy

Read "The Speckled Band" by Sir Arthur Conan Doyle

 Day 3: After You Read

Check Comprehension

1. **Who** is Dr. Grimesby Roylott, and what is his background and reputation?

2. **Why** is Miss Stoner not able to stay in her room?

3. **How** many animals does Dr. Roylott keep on his estate?

Think Critically

"The Speckled Band" is largely considered to be the best Sherlock Holmes short story. This is due in no small part to Sir Arthur Conan Doyle's handpicked list of the best Sherlock stories in which "The Speckled Band" occupies the top spot.

Based on your knowledge of Doyle, why might he have picked this story as the best Sherlock story? Do you agree with him, or would you consider another story the best of Sherlock's adventures?

Write an organized paragraph that explains your answer.

After you understand
what happens in a story and
why it happens, ask yourself,
what's the point?

Main Idea

Sir Arthur Conan Doyle wrote Sherlock Holmes stories to supplement his income so that he could write more "serious" literature; in fact, Doyle himself grew so frustrated with the greater popularity of Sherlock over his other works that he killed off Sherlock in "The Final Problem" in 1893, only to revive him after readers caused an uproar. Doyle clearly did not think of Sherlock as great literature; to him, the famous detective was nothing more than foolish entertainment.

Even if Sherlock stories were written primarily to entertain, can they have a more serious purpose, despite what their author thought of them? Besides entertainment, what could be the main point of a detective story such as "The Speckled Band"? Summarize the main idea in one sentence.

Detective fiction, like science fiction, is generally regarded as non-serious literature, stories people read for fun that do not require much thinking. Is this true of "The Speckled Band"? Support your answer with details from the story or other detective stories you have read.

Analyzing Literature — Mood

A story's *mood* is its atmosphere that elicits a certain response from the reader. Identifying a story's mood can aid the reader in understanding the story.

Although all of a story's elements should support its mood, some parts, such as conversations between characters or observations in the narration, may be particularly helpful in identifying the mood. The way in which characters talk, act, and feel often highlights a story's mood.

Record excerpts from "The Speckled Band" that portray the mood of the story and underline the key words in the excerpt that indicate mood. Then, explain the mood of each excerpt. Finally, using your chosen excerpts as support, write a complete sentence that describes and explains the overall mood.

Excerpt	Explanation
"It is not cold which makes me <u>shiver</u>,' said the woman <u>in a low voice</u>..."	*This excerpt portrays the mood of the story because...*

Mood of "The Speckled Band"
The overall mood of "The Speckled Band" is...

Analyzing Literature activity provided in the Resource Book on page 42.

DIVE DEEPER

1. **Apply** – Using his skills of deductive reasoning, Sherlock helped Miss Stoner by removing the threat of the snake and, subsequently, Dr. Roylott. Other courses of action, however, could have aided her. Using your knowledge of Miss Stoner's situation, construct what could be an alternate solution that is dissimilar to Sherlock's but helps Miss Stoner nonetheless.

2. **Analyze** – *Round characters* are characters who are developed and have complex personalities, emotions, and motives. Classify the round characters of "The Speckled Band"—Dr. Roylott, Miss Stoner, Sherlock, and Watson—as either mostly moral or mostly immoral (e.g., virtuous or wicked) based on their actions throughout the story and explain your reasoning for each choice.

3. **Evaluate** – *Setting* is temporal (relating to time) and physical (relating to location). It can also be used to help discern a story's *mood*. How does the setting of "The Speckled Band" influence the story's mood? Why would a different setting produce a different mood?

 Day 4: After You Read

Analyzing Literature

Foreshadowing is a literary element used to give the readers hints as to what will happen later on in the story. It generally appears at the beginning of a story, and it can come in many forms, such as conversations, events, descriptions of settings or characters, or even the names of characters or places. A famous example of foreshadowing can be found in the Greek tragedy *Oedipus Rex*, when King Oedipus accuses a prophet of being blind, only to be blinded himself later on.

1. Locate the passage in "The Speckled Band" where Dr. Roylott confronts Sherlock in his apartment and demonstrates his strength by bending the fire poker. Consider Sherlock's response after Dr. Roylott leaves and before he straightens out the poker: *"I am not quite so bulky, but if he had remained I might have shown him that my grip was not much more feeble than his own."* What about the men's conversation—and the act of bending and straightening the fire poker—foreshadows their relationship in the rest of the story? Think of the men's interactions, the tense encounter with the snake, and the final outcome of the tale.

Connection Reflection

2. Analyze the strange events in Miss Stoner's home, her following testimony told to Sherlock Holmes, and her reaction to her sister's death. Do you think others, such as her fiancé, have been valid in not believing her story? Would you have believed her? Use details from the text to support your answer.

3. Both Sherlock and Watson risk much to solve this case and save Miss Stoner from her stepfather, even risking death. What was their motivation to act in this way? Would you have done the same that they did? Use details from the text and examples from your own life to support your answer.

Writing Connection

Sherlock Holmes stories are famously narrated by his admiring sidekick, Dr. John Watson. This narration is so famous, in fact, that numerous detective stories copied this narration style and often featured a "Watson" of their own, describing the action through the eyes of an adoring accomplice. The popularity of this practice waned in the mid to late nineteenth century as authors wanted narrators who were either the detectives themselves or who had equal intellectual capabilities as the detectives.

Put aside Dr. Watson for a moment and rewrite the scene in "The Speckled Band" when Dr. Roylott bursts in on Sherlock and Watson from either the perspective of Sherlock Holmes or Dr. Roylott. Imitate the speaking style of whichever character you choose and include their thoughts concerning the current action.

FICTION **49**

 Day 5: After You Read

Nonfiction Connection — Review

The Hollywood trend of adapting popular books and stories rather than creating original content is not a recent one. While many original screenplays flourish, directors and producers often cannot resist the "sure win" of creating a movie based on an already-popular story. Although Sherlock Holmes was created in the nineteenth century, he enjoys popularity in later centuries as well, becoming a favorite of cinematic and theatrical audiences. Consider the Sherlock movies starring Robert Downey Jr. and Jude Law (2009, 2011), or the television series *Sherlock* (2010) and *Elementary* (2012). Even in the twenty-first century, Sherlock still captivates.

Locate the movie review **"The Brave and the Fair, and a Thriller From, the Sherlock Holmes Detective Series. A Conan Doyle Tale. Cinderella Wins Out. A Jolly German Operetta. Those Gangsters Again,"** published by *The New York Times* in 1931.

As you read this review, ask yourself the following questions:
- What is the reviewer's overall opinion of the film?
- Has the reviewer read the original story or not? How do you know?
- What would the reviewer have changed in the film? Do you agree with him?

After you have read the review, think about how you would create an adaptation of "The Speckled Band." Write a paragraph or list of the actors you would choose, the sequence of the story, and the overall mood of your film.

Extended Activities

Watch – Find a film adaptation of "The Speckled Band" on YouTube or another streaming site and watch it with friends or your classmates. (If you cannot find "The Speckled Band," watch an adaptation of another Sherlock Holmes story.) As you watch, consider the following questions: How faithful is the portrayal of the characters to the original story? Does the film have the same mood as the story? What would you change (if anything) about the film?

Research – Determine Sir Arthur Conan Doyle's process of creating Sherlock Holmes stories, especially Sherlock's logical thinking that leads him to his conclusions. Does he work backwards, deciding the outcome and then tracing it back? Does he write the end of the story before the beginning? Research his methods and what he said about writing the Sherlock stories if necessary.

 Complete the Independent Practice on page 44 of the Resource Book.

F) A Worn Path

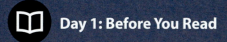
Day 1: Before You Read

WHAT TO LEARN?

- Symbolism
- Monitor
- Biography
- Independent Practice

American Literature

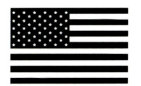

An Uphill CLIMB

Some of the best things is life are difficult to achieve. Friendship is beautiful but also requires effort. Following your dreams is wonderful, but dreams are rarely easy to achieve. Earning good grades in school results from hard work, and winning first place in a competition is necessarily challenging.

As if these things were not difficult enough, life often throws obstacles in your path. A good friend may move to a different state, someone may call your dreams foolish and impossible, a subject in school may prove difficult to understand no matter how much you study, and you may injure yourself and be unable to compete anymore.

What do you do when you encounter obstacles, when life is an uphill climb? Do you press on, or do you turn back? This depends entirely on how valuable your goal is. Some things in life are worth doing no matter how difficult the doing may be.

Meet the Author — Eudora Welty

April 13, 1909–July 23, 2001

An Act of Vision

Welty explored many subjects in her novels and short stories, and she challenged herself by writing each work with different techniques and perspectives. Creating fiction, she said, was "a personal act of vision," and the artist must look squarely at the mysteries of human experience without trying to resolve them. Welty does so through many of her intriguing characters.

Portraits of Empathy

Both a writer and a photographer, Welty sometimes transformed her portraits into fiction, resulting in detailed characters that are treated with gentle empathy. This was especially exemplified in her stories revolving around African Americans. Author Toni Morrison observed that Welty wrote "about black people in a way that few white men have ever been able to write. It's not patronizing, not romanticizing—it's the way they should be written about."

FICTION

F

Day 2: Before You Read

Analyzing Literature — Symbolism

Symbolism is the use of a person, place, object, or action to express a deeper or double meaning, often describing an idea or concept that has no physical attributes. **Symbols** abound in real life, not only fiction. For example, an eagle is an American symbol for the concept of freedom. An olive branch and a white dove are common symbols for peace. A signature on a contract symbolizes that a person agrees to everything stated in the contract.

The use of symbolism adds depth to literature. For example, consider ZZ Packer's short story "Brownies," which focuses on two Girl Scout troops at a camp. One group is composed of only African American girls, and the other is only white girls. The story revolves around the interaction of these two troops, which symbolizes racial prejudice. Even the title "Brownies" functions as a symbol.

Symbolism creates at least two levels of meaning. One is the literal meaning. In "Brownies," two troops get into a fight in a dirty bathroom. One girl starts picking up the trash on the ground. This is what literally happens in the story. Another level of meaning is the symbolic meaning. The fight between the African American troop and the white troop symbolizes racism, and the one girl's picking up trash symbolizes how one person can make a difference to "clean up" the ugliness resulting from racial prejudice. Symbolic meaning applies beyond the immediate situation in a work of literature, leading to widely applicable themes.

Reading Focus: monitor

When reading literature, it is easy to focus on only plot and characters. While these are obviously central to short fiction, themes or important visuals may be subtly imbedded in the writing. *Monitoring* the information you read can train your brain to pick up on these subtleties.

Obstacles	Bird References	Color References
-up a hill -oak woods -a bush snags her dress	-Phoenix's name -"tapping...like the chirping of a solitary little bird"	-"an old Negro woman" -"red rag" -"striped dress"

Reading Focus activity provided in the Resource Book on page 48.

Vocabulary

Sometimes when you encounter new words, you can guess their meaning by thinking of words that are similar. For example, you may not know what hydraulic means, but you can see that it is similar to a fire hydrant. Hydraulic, then, may have something to do with water. When you look it up in the dictionary, you will find that it does.

According to this method, guess the meaning of these vocabulary words from the story. Then look them up in the dictionary to see if you were correct.

phoenix
pendulum
meditative
illumined
quail
pullets
cur
solemn
obstinate

Read "A Worn Path" by Eudora Welty

 Day 3: After You Read

Check Comprehension

1. **How** does Phoenix distract the hunter so she can pick up the nickel?

2. Phoenix does not interact with any relatives during the course of the story. **Why** do the hunter and the people in town call Phoenix "Granny" and "Grandma"?

3. **Why** is Phoenix Jackson going into town?

Think Critically

Some scholars say "A Worn Path" specifically challenges assumptions. After all, the "hero" of the story is a weak old woman. Her being an African American woman is also an upsetting of the usual "heroes" in literature (who often instead resemble the young, white, male hunter Phoenix encounters in the woods).

Each person who encounters Phoenix makes immediate assumptions about her, including the reader. What assumptions did you make about Phoenix at the beginning of the story that were challenged after the story ended? What assumptions did other characters in "A Worn Path" make about Phoenix that were not true? Write an organized paragraph explaining your answers.

After you understand
what happens in a story and
why it happens, ask yourself,
what's the point?

Main Idea

The journey of Phoenix Jackson in "A Worn Path," when read in a symbolic light, illustrates the historical African American experience in the United States, an experience rife with the abuse of slavery and the ugliness of prejudice following the end of slavery. Without this symbolic lens, however, "A Worn Path" is a character study of a woman going to extreme lengths to care for her grandson. Both readings are valid, and both readings focus on perseverance.

What does "A Worn Path" have to say about perseverance? In one complete sentence, describe the central message of this story.

Even though "A Worn Path" focuses on the African American experience, can the story apply to other people groups? In one complete sentence, explain why "A Worn Path" can or cannot apply to more people groups than African Americans.

FICTION

Analyzing Literature — Symbolism

Symbolism is the use of a person, place, object, or action to express a deeper or double meaning, often describing an idea or concept that has no physical attributes. This literary device creates at least two levels of meaning. One is the literal meaning and applies to only the specific characters in an immediate situation. The other level is the symbolic meaning. The symbolic meaning applies beyond the immediate situation in a work of literature, leading to widely applicable themes for any audience.

Many details in "A Worn Path" can act as symbols, but exploring symbolism in literature can be tricky. It is not enough to claim that something acts as a symbol; one must support a claim with evidence from the text or from culture. For example, it is not valid to claim that Phoenix Jackson's journey is a symbol for the American Revolution. Such a claim has no support in the text.

Identify symbols in "A Worn Path." Record details from the text, indicate their symbolic significance, and provide textual support for your interpretation.

What is the symbol in the text?	What does the symbol represent?	How do you know? Textual or cultural support
The slice of marble-cake	African Americans and white people living together and the end of racial prejudice.	The cake is "marble," which means more than one color intertwining. The cake is something desirable, but is not (yet) a reality for Phoenix, just like racial equality.

Analyzing Literature activity provided in the Resource Book on page 50.

DIVE DEEPER

1. **Apply** – The setting of "A Worn Path" is the early 1900s in the rural American south. If the story were to take place today but still communicate the same theme, what would the story be like? Briefly describe what "A Worn Path" would be like in a modern setting. Recreate the main events and conflict and include details like what obstacles Phoenix would face, what her journey is like, and other details.

2. **Analyze** – *Irony* is a contrast or inconsistency between expectations and reality. What is ironic about the hunter's supposition that Phoenix is going into town for the trivial intent "to see Santa Claus"?

3. **Evaluate** – Welty's story is written in third-person limited point of view. Explain how the reader's perception of the other characters would have been altered if the story were told in first-person through Phoenix's eyes. In your opinion, which point of view is best for this story?

Day 4: After You Read

Analyzing Literature

Conflict is the struggle between opposing forces. Conflict in literature can be divided into two broad categories—internal and external conflict. External conflict can be further divided into three specific types:

Person vs. Person	Person vs. Nature
Person vs. Society	

1. Identify an example of each type of external conflict from "A Worn Path."

2. Of the three types of external conflict, which do you think is the most prominent in the story? Why?

Connection Reflection

3. The story reveals that Phoenix Jackson periodically makes this long, hard journey into town to retrieve medicine for her grandson. This distance is so great that even the young and fit hunter declares that it is "too far." Why does Phoenix repeatedly walk this worn path, even though she encounters physical dangers and the disrespect of other people? Explain your answer.

4. Phoenix is not the person who needs the medicine; her grandson is. Yet it is Phoenix who travels the long distance into town over and over again. This is a personal sacrifice on her part. Have you ever had to make a personal sacrifice to help someone else? How did you feel, or how do you imagine you would feel?

Writing Connection

"A Worn Path" can be read as primarily symbolic, but it can also be read as a character study of Phoenix Jackson. As readers journey with Phoenix, not only do they come to know her physical traits, but they are also given the chance to understand her many admirable character traits.

Strong individuals like Phoenix are often the subjects of poetry. Study Phoenix Jackson's character and write a poem about her.

Use figurative language in your poem, such as similes, metaphors, or hyperbole. Decide how much of your poem you want to dedicate to Phoenix's outer characteristics and how much you want to dedicate to her inner characteristics.

 Day 5: After You Read

Nonfiction Connection

Biography

Welty's short story "A Worn Path" is a narrative about a woman who overcomes obstacle after obstacle to reach a goal she considers worth the pain and hardship. Phoenix Jackson is a fictional character, but her story is similar to many people's real-life experiences. Every day, ordinary people often struggle to accomplish their goals. They have to overcome obstacles that others do not, including prejudice against one's race, religion, gender, culture, body type, and many other stereotypes.

Throughout history, cultures have suppressed the stories of people who were thought of as inferior. The disrespectful attitudes Phoenix Jackson encounters on her journey reflect only a small amount of the disrespect African Americans have endured over the course of history. In an effort to mend the wounds inflicted for centuries, people have been telling those stories once stifled by prejudice.

Look up **"Five African-Americans Forgotten in History" by Joe McGasko.**

As you read,
- keep track of the obstacles each person faced in their personal journeys.
- keep track of the goals each person had in mind.
- note what each individual ended up achieving in the long run.

If you had the opportunity to learn more about Mary Ellen Pleasant, Bessie Coleman, Jesse LeRoy Brown, Matthew Henson, William H. Hastie, or even the fictional Phoenix Jackson, whom would you choose? Why would you choose that person?

Write an organized paragraph explaining your answers or discuss your answers with your teacher or fellow students.

Extended Activities

Hiking – Find a national park or hiking trail near you. Take a trip with your family or friends and hike a trail. Observe your surroundings. If there was not a predetermined path for you, how easy would it be to travel through the environment? As you hike, remember old Phoenix Jackson traveling through woods and fields on a path only she knows.

Volunteer – Phoenix did everything she could to bring soothing medicine to her grandson, who could not help himself. Volunteer to serve at a local social program or hospital. As you serve other people, remember Phoenix's service to her grandson.

 Complete the Independent Practice on page 52 of the Resource Book.

Complete Fiction Unit Summative Assessment

Fiction Summative Assessment is provided in the Resource Book on page 56.

Drama Unit

The Literature You'll Read:

Susan Glaspell	Trifles
Anton Chekov	The Boor
O. Henry	*While the Auto Waits

The Concepts You'll Study:

Analyzing Literature
Plot
Irony
Dynamic Characters

Drama Focus
Visualize
Making Inferences

Writing Connection
Review
Modernizing Language

Theatrical Connection
Set Design
Casting

*Summative Assessment

Exploring Literature  Day 1

Drama

Reading is an individual experience. Even if thousands of people read the same book or short story, they will each process the story through their own individual imaginations. Drama, on the other hand, is a community experience. Not only does it require a community of people to produce a theatrical production, but playgoers will experience the drama as a group—as one audience.

As a genre of literature, drama is a play for the theater, radio, or film (but this unit explores theater). A playwright crafts a story into a script, which is then interpreted by directors and designers and performed by actors and actresses, all funded and governed by a producer. Sets are constructed, costumes are created, and sometimes music and sound effects are used during a production.

> To produce a drama, a large group of people work together to create an immersive experience that takes place in real time in a 3-D setting that appeals to physical senses as well as imagination.

The audience (playgoers) is also a vital part of the theatrical experience. After meeting the characters at the start of the play, the audience starts to look for the solution to whatever problem is introduced. The audience creeps to the edge of their seats as tension builds, and they hold their breath as the climax breaks upon them. Then, everyone can finally breathe again, and they are prepared to reenter the real world—hopefully impacted for the better—as the play closes.

> When attending a drama, people get the chance to come together, laugh as a unit, cry collectively, and experience all the tension and emotion of a story as one group.

Plays are not short stories; they are meant to be performed, not simply read. The script is only a starting point. Reading a play will not provide the same immersive experience as attending a live production, but a drama can still be appreciated and analyzed by reading its script.

DRAMA 59

LITERARY ELEMENTS

Fiction is meant to be read, and drama is meant to be performed. Even with this vital difference, both fiction and drama tell stories and utilize the same elements of literature to do so.

Plot is a series of events that revolves around a central conflict.

The stages of plot include **exposition, rising action, climax, falling action,** and **resolution.**

Conflict is a struggle between opposing forces.

In **external conflict**, a character struggles with an outside force, usually another person, a force of nature, or an element of society. In **internal conflict**, a character struggles inside their own heart or mind.

Characters are the people around whom the plot and conflict revolve.

Main characters are central to a plot and vital to the focal conflict. *Minor characters* may move the plot along but are not fundamental to the story. Characters can also be described as either *flat* (undeveloped) or *round* (developed) as well as *dynamic* (they undergo a change) or *static* (they do not change).

Setting is a series of events that revolves around a central conflict.

Temporal setting involves time, and *physical setting* involves the location.

Theme is a pervasive meaning woven throughout a piece of literature.

Repeated elements, symbols, and what is portrayed positively and negatively in a work can all help reveal a drama's theme. Other places to find theme are in the title of a work, how the characters act and what they say, and how the conflict is resolved.

Mood is the prevalent emotion that the audience feels while watching a play.

Mood is not entirely dependent on subject matter but is dependent on how the subject matter is treated through the environment, acting, and dialogue.

Tone is a playwright's attitude toward their own story.

Does the playwright treat their subject matter comically or seriously? What is treated positively and negatively? The answers to these questions determine the tone of a work.

Irony is a contrast or inconsistency between expectations and reality.

Something in literature is ironic when what occurs is different than what the reader or the characters expected.
Verbal irony is when something a character says means something different or more than what the words seem to mean.
Situational irony is when the outcome of a situation is different than what was expected.
Dramatic irony is when the audience knows something the characters do not know.

Foreshadowing is a warning or indication of a future event; a hint at what is to come in the story.

Readers usually do not understand foreshadowing elements until they read or watch the play a second time.

Symbolism is the use of a person, place, object, or action to express a deeper or double meaning, often describing an idea or concept that has no physical attributes.

Symbolism creates at least two levels of meaning: the literal meaning that applies only to the plot of the story, and the symbolic meaning that applies beyond the immediate situation and leads to widely applicable themes.

DRAMA

D  Day 3

ELEMENTS OF DRAMA

Even though drama contains the same literary elements as fiction, these elements are treated in a unique way when presented in dramatic format. Drama also has a few unique aspects.

Plot

The action of a play is experienced from start to finish in one sitting. Every action and event must be a vital contribution to what happens next and the overall plot, for in a live performance, there is no time to waste. Unlike short stories and novels, which can be put aside by the reader and picked up again later, an audience in a theater has no option to "pick up" the play later. Fiction can meander, but drama gets down to business.

> One-act plays are anywhere between fifteen to thirty minutes long, while multi-act plays can be two to four hours in length.

Conflict

If drama contains all the same types of conflict that fiction does, how are the various types of conflict communicated on stage? In fiction, a narrator can explain that certain external conflicts exist, such as how one character does not get along with another, how a family does not have enough money to pay their bills, or how a child is afraid of storms. In drama, however, there is no narrator (in most cases). Thus, external conflict must be communicated through what can be seen or heard.

A woman is sitting at a diner counter. A man enters, they see each other, and each groans. The woman turns her back to the man and faces the other way.	*A man in dirty clothes slogs into a sparsely furnished house. He calls out "Shannon?" A woman enters from the kitchen wearing worn clothes. The lights flicker and go out. The man sighs in defeat. The woman says, "Don't worry. We have candles, and it's summer. We don't need electricity this month anyway."*	*A child sits on a sofa. The lighting is dark. Through the front door enters a woman, and a low rumble is heard. The child squeals and curls up, hiding his face. The woman hurries to the couch, saying, "It's okay, honey. It's just a little thunder, and Mommy is here."*
The characters' reactions to each other reveal to the audience that they do not get along.	The costuming, the set, and the woman's dialogue all imply that this family has very little money and did not pay their electric bill.	The sound and lighting indicate that a storm is brewing, and the child's reaction coupled with the woman's response demonstrate the child's fear.

But what about internal conflict? How can a character's internal struggles be communicated onstage to an audience? Sometimes playwrights make their characters speak their thoughts out loud so the audience can understand what is going on inside their minds. Audience members can also watch characters' actions and listen to how they speak their dialogue. Sometimes, a character's inaction or silence can also be an indication of internal conflict.

> A young adult is sitting on her mattress, holding letters in each hand. She looks between the two, frowning. Looking at one paper, she sighs and says, "M State," and then looks at the other paper and says, "or you." She lays both pages on her bed and carefully flattens each out. She crosses her arms, still looking between the letters, before groaning, falling back, and covering her head with her pillow.

The minimal dialogue reveals that the young adult must make a choice about where to go to college. Her movements then indicate that she is struggling to make the choice.

Setting

With just the power of imagination, fiction can take the readers through many locations as well as across time—jumping from one day to the next or even a week or a year later. While imagination is still a requirement when viewing a play, the physical setting must be contained within the stage. This creates certain restrictions and challenges when it comes to a drama's setting.

Setting—both temporal and physical—is communicated through the set and scenery, and the set and scenery must be constructed and take up a finite space.

While a short story or novel can take characters from the streets of New York City to a small-town rodeo to a penthouse in London all in the same story, such dramatic shifts in setting are virtually impossible on a stage. Dramas typically take place in very few settings, sometimes even only one. If, for some reason, the physical or temporal setting must change for the sake of the story, the change must take place swiftly and easily; after all, the audience is sitting in the dark, waiting for the story to continue. Therefore, setting is usually suggested through a few key physical elements rather than a completely accurate representation of the setting.

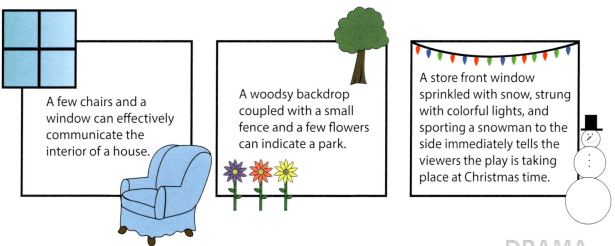

A few chairs and a window can effectively communicate the interior of a house.

A woodsy backdrop coupled with a small fence and a few flowers can indicate a park.

A store front window sprinkled with snow, strung with colorful lights, and sporting a snowman to the side immediately tells the viewers the play is taking place at Christmas time.

DRAMA

Characters

The beginning of a script contains brief descriptions of each person in a play, including names and sometimes indicating age, appearance, and any relationships with other characters (mother, brother, aunt, etc.). An audience, however, will not have access to the script. All this information must be revealed to them through the action and dialogue as well as the setting and props.

A young man lounges in a chair, looking at a laptop and wearing headphones. He is in a bedroom with movie posters on the wall, sports trophies on the shelf, a backpack near the door, and crumpled laundry all about the floor.

The setting and the young man's activity reveal that this character is probably a teenager.

A woman sits on a couch folding clothes. Off-stage, a young woman's voice calls, "We're out of milk!" The woman on the couch answers, "I'll get some tomorrow—No! Text your father and ask if he'll pick some up!"

The woman's actions and setting reveal that she is probably a mother, and the conversation between her and the unseen young woman indicates that the young woman is probably her daughter.

A character's defining characteristics (traits) must also be communicated through wardrobe, dialogue, and action. No narrator is used to tell the audience what the characters are like. What can you infer about these characters based on their dress, words, and movements?

A man in a suit enters a mechanic's garage. Glancing around the garage, he ventures to a corner far away from all the dirty surfaces and checks his cuffs. After looking around with small movements of his head, he clears his throat and adjusts his tie. Clasping his hands in front of him, he stands still and straight as a telephone pole.

A woman enters a kitchen, followed by another woman, both with arms laden with groceries. The first woman has her hair hastily pulled up into an unruly bun, and she enters the room talking: "So she said, 'Don't even go there,' and I said, 'I will go there if I want to!' and she said, 'Why you gotta be so dramatic?' and I said, 'Dramatic? I ain't dramatic, I'm just right and you know it!' Some people, I tell ya, some people..."

An old man sits in a big armchair, covered in a blanket and apparently sleeping. An old woman enters, sees the man, and quietly closes the door behind her. She goes to the man and adjusts the blanket in his lap before leaning forward and kissing the top of his head. She stands and looks down at him for a moment, a smile on her face. She then proceeds to straighten the pillows on the nearby couch.

Language

What words are spoken and how they are spoken immensely affect the atmosphere of a play. Sometimes, actors will need to deliver their lines with a certain accent, for the accent can indicate the setting (physical or temporal). Word choice is also important because certain classes of people have a certain vocabulary. A Wall Street broker probably would not use the word "reckon," and a Midwestern farmer probably would not use the word "fortuitous" in regular conversation.

Because the audience is listening to the dialogue—and not just reading it, as with fiction—the audience gets to know the characters through their vocabulary and enunciation, just like in real life.

Music

The sound of a dramatic production—including background noises, sound effects, and instrumentals—also affects the atmosphere of a play, and it is a distinctive feature of drama. Fiction cannot include music as part of the storytelling experience, but drama can.

Music can be used to heighten intensity, indicate mood, and sometimes—in the case of musical dramas—push the plot forward. Not every play utilizes music, but it is a special tool available to dramatists. Producers must be careful, however, that any music or sound effects they use do not distract the audience or drown out vital dialogue.

Spectacle

The spectacle of a theater includes all visual aspects of the drama, meaning the scenery, the props, the wardrobe, and any special effects. Some plays are flashy, bedazzling events, and others reflect real-life conditions as best they can. If the spectacle of a play uses mostly drab colors, crooked shapes, and harsh lighting, the atmosphere of the theater may be spooky or dismal. In contrast, if the spectacle of a play utilizes vibrant colors, cartoonish backdrops, and outrageous costumes, the mood of the production would be lighthearted and possibly comical.

DRAMA

HOW TO READ A PLAY

Reading a drama for the first time may be difficult because scripts for plays are presented very differently on the page than short stories. The text of a play consists mostly of dialogue with very little else. Therefore, using one's imagination while reading is vital in order to effectively visualize the story. As you read a script, imagine what the characters are doing, how they would deliver their lines, and what the setting looks like.

Each script may differ slightly, but generally, the first page looks like this:

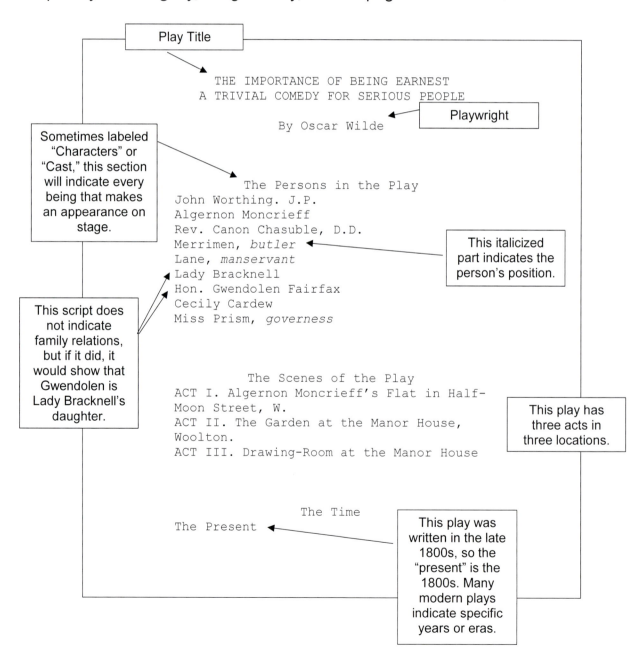

The rest of the pages in a script look like this:

> Here is the only description of setting in the script. If the setting changes from scene to scene, then it will be indicated here at the beginning of the scene.

FIRST ACT

SCENE: *Morning-room in Algernon's flat in Half-Moon Street. The room is luxuriously and artistically furnished. The sound of a piano is heard in the adjoining room.*

[Lane is arranging afternoon tea on the table, and after the music has ceased, Algernon enters.]

Algernon: Did you hear what I was playing, Lane?

Lane: I didn't think it polite to listen, sir.

Algernon: I'm sorry for that, for your sake. I don't play accurately—any one can play accurately—but I play with wonderful expression. As far as the piano is concerned, sentiment is my forte. I keep science for Life.

Lane: Yes, sir.

Algernon: And, speaking of the science of Life, have you got the cucumber sandwiches cut for Lady Bracknell?

Lane: Yes, sir. *[Hands them on a salver.]*

Algernon: *[Inspects them, takes two, and sits down on the sofa.]* Oh! ... by the way, Lane, I see from your book that on Thursday night, when Lord Shoreman and Mr. Worthing were dining with me, eight bottles of champagne are entered as having been consumed.

Lane: Yes, sir; eight bottles and a pint.

> Action is indicated in brackets.

> Algernon appears on stage, probably entering through a doorway.

> No "he said" or "she said" is used in a script. Whenever a character speaks, their dialogue is included just after their name.

> Bracketed action that is included in the same line as dialogue indicates that the character does the action while speaking. This is a called a "stage direction."

DRAMA

D

▶ Day 6

THEATER TERMS

Every profession and field of study has its own important terms and vocabulary. Drama is no different.

People of the Theater

Actors/actresses – Men/women who portray characters in a performance. They may be referred to collectively as "actors."

Designers – The people who design and create the physical apects of a play, such as a set designer, a costume designer, and a sound designer.

Director – The person who oversees and orchestrates a theatrical production, making sure that all efforts and aspects work together to create a unified drama.

Playwright – The person who writes plays. "Wright" is a word for a craftsperson or someone who builds things.

Producer – The person who oversees all financial and managerial functions of a production, keeping track of money spent and earned, as well as hiring all other positions. Sometimes the "producer" of a play is an institution, such as a university.

Stage crew – The group of people that operates the technical aspects of a play during a performance, such as scene changes, prop placement, costume changes, lighting, sound, etc.

Stage manager – The person who coordinates all aspects of a theater company, such as rehearsals, actors, and props. The stage manager makes sure everything the director wants and the producer paid for works successfully.

68

Physical Parts of a Theater

House/audience – Where the audience sits during a performance. "Facing the house" means "facing the seats of the theater."

Props – Any moveable object used by actors onstage during a performance.

Set – The representation of setting on a stage, including the scenery and other large objects (like furniture or a fake wall).

Staging – The process of designing the performance space for a play, including how actors will move about the set and where to place props and bits of scenery.

Stage right/left – Stage right and left use the perspective of an actor facing the audience; therefore, stage right and left are opposite to the right and left of the audience.

Terms Associated with Drama Scripts

Act – A large division of a play usually divided according to the stages of plot.

Cast – All actors and extras needed on stage at any point during the play.

Exits and entrances – An actor "exits" when they are no longer visible on stage, and an actor "enters" when they become visible on stage.

Scene – A small division of a play including actions that happen all in the same time and place.

Stage direction – Notes in the script that tell actors how to move or deliver their lines.

D. Trifles

Day 1: Before You Read

WHAT TO LEARN?
- Plot
- Visualizing
- Independent Practice

We live close together and *we live* far apart

What is happening behind the closed door down the hall? Or behind the fence down the street in your neighborhood? Or in the next town over? Or across the world in another country? Every person on the planet experiences life in their own way, with joy and pain and friends and enemies and choices and consequences. It is impossible to know what someone else is going through…or is it?

Even though all people have individual life stories, they are still very similar in many ways. Everyone knows what it feels like to be frightened as well as how difficult it is to be brave. No one likes to be lonely, and everyone is in need of friends. We do not always see the similarities between ourselves and other people, but then again, we do not always look.

In *Trifles*, a group of men and women are given the chance to peer into the life of a woman named Mrs. Wright. While some of the characters are not interested in understanding her, others look with empathy and discover common ground.

American Literature

Meet the Author — Susan Glaspell

July 1, 1876–July 28, 1948

A Woman Reporter
The day after Glaspell graduated from college, she became a full-time reporter for the newspaper—a rare position for a woman at the time. Glaspell was often assigned to cover murder cases. When she was twenty-four, however, she resigned her position and moved away; this abrupt change occurred just after she covered the conviction of a woman accused of murdering her abusive husband.

Groundbreaking Playwright
Glaspell is not only considered a great feminist pioneer but is also regarded as a genius writer regardless of gender. She wrote many dramatic masterpieces as well as novels and short stories. Her first play, *Trifles*, is one of the most studied works of American theatre, challenging audiences with its views of justice and morality. She later adapted the play into a short story called "A Jury of Her Peers."

Analyzing Literature — Plot

Some more experimental plays attempt to create dramas that are **plotless**, such as the famous existential play *Waiting for Godot* by Samuel Beckett, in which essentially nothing happens. Excepting such avant-garde pieces of literature, most dramas have a **plot**—a series of events the revolve around a central conflict.

The stages of plot for a play are the same as they are for short stories.
- *Exposition* – The characters and setting are established, and the main conflict is introduced.
- *Rising Action* – The characters try to solve the conflict, and the tension of a story builds.
- *Climax* – The conflict is at its most intense, and the outcome of the story is decided.
- *Falling Action* – The conflict is resolved, and all loose ends are tied up.
- *Resolution* – The outcome of the main conflict is revealed.

Plays are not short stories; they are meant to be performed, not simply read. After meeting the characters in the exposition, the audience starts to look for the solution to whatever problem is introduced. The audience creeps to the edge of their seats as tension builds during the rising action, and they hold their breath as the climax breaks upon them. Viewers can finally breathe again during the falling action and are prepared to reenter the real world through the resolution.

Reading a play will not provide the same immersive experience as attending a live production, but the stages of plot can still be identified in the text of the script.

Drama Focus: visualizing

In some scripts, the setting and characters are described in detail; in others, they are only given general descriptions. The set designer, actors, and director often make their own creative decisions about how to perform the play. Reading the text of a drama will not offer the complete experience of a play, so readers must use their imaginations to **visualize** what we might see in a live performance.

Using the descriptions in the script and your own imagination, describe the various dramatic elements of the play *Trifles* in the boxes provided.

Set	Props	Actors	Wardrobe

Drama Focus activity provided in the Resource Book on page 67.

Read "Trifles" by Susan Glaspell

Day 3: After You Read

Check Comprehension

1. **Why** are Mrs. Peters and Mrs. Hale at the house with the men?

2. **What** was Mrs. Wright's name before she married?

3. **When** the ladies examine Mrs. Wright's quilting squares, what do they think the portion with uneven stitching indicates?

4. The men say everything is clear except for one thing. **What** is that one thing?

Think Critically

Because it seems as though not much happens in the play, scholars say that the key to *Trifles* is understanding the irony and symbolism in the play. **Symbolism** is the use of a person, place, object, or action to express a deeper or double meaning. Scholars claim that the jam preserves, broken by the cold weather, symbolize Minnie Foster. Minnie was a sweet girl before she married, but her spirit was broken by the coldness of Mr. Wright.

Many also view the dead canary as a symbol of Minnie Foster. Why would scholars associate the bird with Minnie? Is this symbolism important to the story?

Write an organized paragraph explaining your answers, using details from the text as support.

After you read a script, think about the **physical actions** actors must perform to create the **emotional atmosphere** of the play.

In the Audience

A play is an immersive experience—much more than words on a page. The scenery on the stage is built to give the illusion that the setting of the play is real. Audience members watch the actors move about the set and interact with each other, and the lighting shifts to accentuate the mood of a scene. Playgoers also listen to the actors raise and lower their voices and speak their dialogue in a certain manner. The script guides these creative decisions made by those putting on a play, helping them to portray the proper emotional atmosphere for a story.

If you were in the audience during a production of *Trifles*, what would be the emotional atmosphere of the theater during the performance? What physical actions might the players perform that would indicate to you, an audience member, the mood of the play?

DRAMA

Analyzing Literature

Plot

The Stages of Plot
- *Exposition* – The characters and setting are established, and the main conflict is introduced.
- *Rising Action* – The characters try to solve the conflict, and the tension of a story builds.
- *Climax* – The conflict is at its most intense, and the outcome of the story is decided.
- *Falling Action* – The conflict is resolved, and all loose ends are tied up.
- *Resolution* – The outcome of the main conflict is revealed.

Even though *Trifles* does not have much action, the play still has a plot that follows Mrs. Hale and Mrs. Peters. The play also has a secondary plot, as many mysteries do: the series of events involving Minnie Foster that leads up to the crime. The main plot of the play reveals the secondary plot of the crime as Mrs. Hale and Mrs. Peters uncover evidence. Consider how the climaxes for the two plots are similar and different.

Identify the stages of plot for both the main plot and the secondary plot. Use information gained from the dialogue and discoveries to piece together the events that lead up to the murder in the secondary plot.

Main Plot (involving Mrs. Hale and Mrs. Peters)	Secondary Plot (involving Minnie Foster and the crime)
Exposition: …	Exposition: …
Rising Action: …	Rising Action: …
…	…

Analyzing Literature activity provided in the Resource Book on page 68.

DIVE DEEPER

1. **Apply** – *Motives* are characters' reasons for doing what they do. Succinctly explain what Mrs. Hale and Mrs. Peters believe motivated the murder of Mr. Wright.

2. **Analyze** – Everyone thinks that strangling Mr. Wright with a rope was a "funny way to kill a man." Explain the importance of the way Mr. Wright was murdered.

3. **Evaluate** – Mrs. Hale and Mrs. Peters choose not to share their findings with the sheriff and the other men. If they had, however, how do you think the men would have reacted, considering how the men treat the concerns of women throughout the play?

Day 4: After You Read

Analyzing Literature

In literature, irony is a contrast or inconsistency between expectations and reality.
- *Verbal irony*—when something a character says is different than what the character means (whether or not the character realizes this)
- *Situational irony*—when the outcome of a situation is different than what the characters or the audience expected
- *Dramatic irony*—when the audience knows something the characters in a story do not know

1. The men search for evidence of a motive but are not at all interested in the kitchen. The sheriff says there's "nothing here but kitchen things." How does this statement demonstrate verbal irony?

2. The title of the play comes from Mr. Hale's line "women are used to worrying over trifles." This line summarizes how the men view the women in the play. How does the title *Trifles* function ironically? Explain your answer using evidence from the text.

Connection Reflection

3. Do you agree with Mrs. Hale and Mrs. Peter's choice to hide the truth? If you were in their position, what would you have done? Why?

4. Whether or not you agree with Mrs. Wright's actions, can you understand her motives? Why do you think she felt so strongly about such a "little thing" as a dead bird?

Writing Connection

A *review* is a personal but educated response to a dramatic performance, either in film or a live drama. Reviews have 5 main parts:

Introduction	Execution	Specifics	Opinion	Recommendation
What is the play, and who is producing it?	How is the play executed well or poorly?	What about this production is worth noting specifically?	What about the production worked, and what did not?	Is this production worth seeing? Why or why not?

Many recordings of *Trifles* performances are available on YouTube. Some are stage productions, and some are independent films. (Some are called "A Jury of Her Peers.") Choose a performance, watch it, and write a review of the production.

 Day 5: After You Read

Theatrical Connection — Set Design

When producing a drama, much more goes into the production than just the script. One of the important parts of dramatic production is **set design**. A set designer establishes the visual concept of a production—what audiences see. A quality set designer will create an environment that is fitting for each play, for a play like Shakespeare's *Romeo and Juliet* will require a very different environment than a musical like *Oklahoma!* by Rodgers and Hammerstein.

One of the jobs of a set designer is to create a **basic ground plan**. This shows where all the stationary scenic elements go on a stage. A basic ground plan must take into account:
- what audiences can and cannot see
- exit and entrance points for the actors
- how the actors must move around the scene
- where to place important props for the actors to interact with

Susan Glaspell's one-act play requires only one set design. Create a basic ground plan for *Trifles*.

As you design,
- skim the script of the play. Note the stage directions and any time the characters interact with the environment (such as going in and out of doors, up or down stairs, looking in cabinets, sitting down, etc.). Include these elements in your design.
- keep in mind that actors need to move about the stage with ease.
- remember that the audience must be able to see everything.
- look up how other plays have been staged to help guide you.

A "Blank Stage" sheet is included in the Resource Book on page 70.

Extended Activities

Crafting – Quilting is a craft that requires sewing, design, and geometry skills. Design and create a quilting square, just like Minnie Foster's quilting squares.

Reading – Find and read the short fiction adaptation of *Trifles*, called "A Jury of Her Peers." How is the short story different from the stage play?

STOP Complete the Independent Practice on page 72 of the Resource Book.

D. The Boor

📖 Day 1: Before You Read

WHAT TO LEARN?
- Verbal Irony
- Making Inferences
- Independent Practice

You know what I MEANT to say

Have you ever experienced trouble when trying to express your opinion or tell a story? Maybe you have said something that sounded innocent to you but was misinterpreted by your listeners, or perhaps you have found it difficult to put your feelings into words.

Even though we use it every day, language is a tricky thing and often complicates our relationships with others. We may intentionally hide how we feel by using deceiving language, or we may unintentionally confuse situations by using vague language. Sometimes, we are not aware that our family or friends have misinterpreted us or that we have misinterpreted others, which causes trouble either immediately or later on.

Have you ever misinterpreted what someone told you or been misunderstood by someone else? What was the result of the misunderstanding? Did it affect your relationship with the other person? Discuss your answers with your teacher or fellow students.

World Literature

Meet the Author — Anton Chekhov

A Modern Man

Chekhov is credited as one of the pioneers of modernism (an artistic movement that defies classical and traditional norms) in the theatre, often puzzling audiences with his innovations in literature. He made no apologies, commenting that "the role of the artist is to ask questions, not answer them."

An Accidental Genius

Famous for his short stories and plays, Chekhov began writing not out of a love for literature but to provide income for his family, which had been made poor after Chekhov's father was cheated by a contractor and overextended his finances. As Chekhov continued to write, however, his works became more literary and showed talent, attracting critical praise from other prominent writers and prompting Chekhov to take his writing more seriously.

29 Jan 1860–15 July 1904

Analyzing Literature

Verbal Irony

Irony is a contrast or inconsistency between expectations and reality. It is the difference between what the characters or the audience expect to happen and what actually happens.

While coincidence is often mistaken for irony, the two concepts are not interchangeable. Unexpectedly seeing an old friend you were thinking about is not ironic; it is coincidental. Not being able to go on a picnic because of rain is not ironic; it is coincidental. Irony requires the occurrence of something that is the opposite of what was expected.

One type of irony in literature is **verbal irony**, which is when what a character says means the opposite of or something greater than what it seems. Verbal irony can be intentional or unintentional depending on how self-aware the character is. In Shakespeare's *Othello*, Othello praises his friend Iago for his honesty. However, he is unaware that Iago is plotting to make Othello's wife appear unfaithful, which will cause chaos. When Othello says Iago is a man "of honesty and trust," his words are verbally ironic.

Drama Focus: making inferences

Unlike short stories or novels, which give the reader additional explanation about what is happening through narration, plays depend primarily on dialogue to convey information to the audience. Because of this, making inferences is an important part of reading a script or watching a drama. Unless the play uses a narrator, nothing directly tells the audience exactly what is happening or what something means. Therefore, the audience must infer from the dialogue and action how the characters feel and what they think. Making inferences is especially important when a playwright uses verbal irony.

As you read, make inferences about what Mrs. Popov and Mr. Smirnov say compared to what they actually mean. Record their words and their actions in the first column and your inferences in the second column.

Dialogue with Actions	Inference
Mr. Smirnov asserts that men, not women, are the ones who are true and faithful in love. Mrs. Popov says, "The man true and faithful in love! Well, that is something new!"	Mrs. Popov is mocking Mr. Smirnov's view of men. She is saying that men are not true and faithful in love.

Drama Focus activity provided in the Resource Book on page 76.

Read "The Boor" by Anton Chekhov

Day 3: After You Read

Check Comprehension

1. **Who** is Luka? What is his connection to Mrs. Popov?

2. **Why** does Mr. Smirnov refuse to leave when Mrs. Popov asks him to?

3. **What** event at the end of the play shocks Mrs. Popov's household?

Think Critically

Originally, Anton Chekhov thought little of *The Boor*, writing to a friend that he had written "a trivial little vaudeville" to "while away the time." In the same letter, he worried that critics would dismiss him as a inconsequential author because of the play, but audiences proved him wrong: from the first performance, *The Boor* was a success, garnering large audiences and providing Chekhov with recurring royalties (fees for permission to use his play) throughout his lifetime.

Why might *The Boor* have been so popular and so well received, even though Chekhov himself considered it to be little more than a humorous distraction? What might audiences have found likeable and enduring about the play?

Write an organized paragraph that explains your answer.

After you read a script, think about the **physical actions** actors must perform to create the **emotional atmosphere** of the play.

In the Audience

A play is an immersive experience—much more than words on a page. Playgoers must listen carefully to dialogue, for once a line has been said, the actors move on to the next. Playgoers must also carefully observe the facial expressions and subtle actions of the actors, inferring their importance and their portrayal of the respective characters.

A playgoer must also learn to focus on multiple aspects of the play at the same time, for if a playgoer does not pay attention, they might miss a crucial piece of information given by a character or implied by their actions. Plays are driven by dialogue and supplemented with actions; because of this, understanding the balance of dialogue and action is vital to experiencing a play in the fullest manner possible.

A

If you were in the audience for a production of *The Boor*, how would you balance paying attention to the dialogue and to the actions? How would you keep track of everything happening in the play, making sure that you are missing nothing? Write an organized paragraph that explains your answer.

DRAMA

Analyzing Literature

Verbal Irony

Irony is a contrast or inconsistency between expectations and reality. It is the difference between what the characters or the audience expect to happen and what actually happens.

When characters say the opposite of what they mean, the opposite of what is true, or layer their words with double meanings, **verbal irony** occurs. They may be aware that they are speaking ironically, or they may be unaware that what they are saying is ironic or untrue.

Record excerpts from Mrs. Popov and Mr. Smirnov's lines in *The Boor* that demonstrate verbal irony. Then, explain why the excerpts you chose are examples of verbal irony. (Hint: think about how both characters truly feel as opposed to what they say.)

What do the characters say?	Why is this verbal irony?
Mrs. Popov: No, go on, go on, I hate you.	Mrs. Popov doesn't really want Mr. Smirnov to leave, for she immediately tells him to stay after she says she hates him.

Analyzing Literature activity provided in the Resource Book on page 78.

DIVE DEEPER

1. **Apply** – *The Boor* is a one-act play in which the events occur in one room. The setting of a play is crucial for helping create its mood. Sketch a visual representation of the set, including furniture and props, designing it however you wish. Then, write a few sentences explaining why you chose to portray the set in such a manner.

2. **Analyze** – Mrs. Popov and Mr. Smirnov's personalities clash for the majority of the play, providing the main conflict of the plot. Compare the two characters and examine their similarities. Why might their similarities in personality cause them to fight with each other?

3. **Evaluate** – Assess Mrs. Popov's initial view of men and Mr. Smirnov's initial view of women. Does either view hold merit? Is one wrong? Are both wrong? Explain your answer using details from the text, paying special attention to pertinent dialogue from the two characters.

 Day 4: After You Read

Analyzing Literature

In literature, a **dynamic character** is a character who changes or grows in some way before the end of the story, usually as the result of a significant event or relationship. The opposite of this character is the **static character**, who does not change at all throughout the course of the story.

Do not confuse dynamic characters with **round characters**, or developed characters. A dynamic character is generally a round character, but a round character is not always a dynamic character. A character can be round without changing in some way.

1. Identify one dynamic character and one static character in *The Boor*. What makes each character dynamic or static?

2. Is it possible for a play or another piece of literature to include only static characters? Why or why not?

Connection Reflection

3. The main characters in *The Boor*, Mrs. Popov and Mr. Smirnov, are examples of *alazons*, a Greek theatre term for characters who think they are greater or nobler than they actually are. Mrs. Popov frequently mentions that she is mourning her dead husband and therefore will not see other men, yet she finds herself attracted to Mr. Smirnov within a short while. Mr. Smirnov professes to hate women, yet he is drawn to Mrs. Popov's dimples and her seemingly-extraordinary character. What is Chekhov trying to say about human nature through alazons such as Mrs. Popov and Mr. Smirnov? Explain your answer using details from the play.

Writing Connection

The Boor was written in 1888, and its language and setting reflect the time period in which it was written. Choose a portion of the play (or the entire play, if you are feeling adventurous) and rewrite it in modern language, giving modern situations to Mrs. Popov and Mr. Smirnov. You may also set the play in a different location, if you prefer. As you rewrite your portion, consider what you must change in order to modernize it and what may remain the same.

Theatrical Connection — Casting

The Boor is a one-act play with three main characters and a few supporting characters. Of the three main characters, the play focuses on Mrs. Popov and Mr. Smirnov, whose interactions and disagreements compose the majority of the play.

Casting (choosing a cast) is an important part of producing a play, for actors who accurately portray the play's characters need to be chosen in order to make the play effective. A tall, thin man would make an unconvincing Mr. Smirnov, for example, and a seventy-year-old woman would not be a good choice for Mrs. Popov. Most casting directors will choose actors for a play according to how the characters are described by the playwright in the script.

Imagine you are the casting director for an onstage production of *The Boor*. Assemble your main cast for the play (Mrs. Popov, Mr. Smirnov, and Luka).

1. Assemble an ideal cast of professional actors. Support each choice with reasons why the actor is a good fit for the role.

2. Assemble a different cast, this one consisting of people you know, such as friends and family members. Again, support each choice with reasons why the person is a good fit.

Note: theatrical acting is a different process than cinematic acting; it is the difference between acting to an audience and acting to a screen. This may influence your casting decisions. For the first list, you may want to choose from actors who have experience acting in the theater instead of actors who have cinematic experience only.

Extended Activities

Attending – Research local plays or musicals that are being performed in your area and, if possible, attend a production of one with a few classmates or friends. Try to observe every aspect of the play—the actors' interactions with one another, the set design, the choice of props, etc. Take notes during the play of what the actors, designers, and director did well and what could have been improved. After the play, discuss with your fellow playgoers what you would have changed and what you would have kept the same.

Designing – A *prop* (short for "property") is an item used by actors or on a set to lend credibility to a stage production. Props can be realistic, such as a real book, or exaggerated, such as an enlarged book made of posterboard. Gather or create props that could be used in a production of *The Boor*. Read through the play again to determine the props you need.

STOP Complete the Independent Practice on page 80 of the Resource Book.

Complete Drama Unit Summative Assessment

Drama Summative Assessment is provided in the Resource Book on page 84.

Performing a Drama
Production Project

Plays are meant to be performed and viewed, not simply read. The script is only a starting point.

Attending a dramatic performance is one way to experience a play, but another way is to participate in the performance yourself. Making creative decisions about how to best construct the set, direct the action, and deliver the dialogue can give you a deeper understanding and appreciation for the dramatic arts.

*NOTE: After completing the Summative Assessment, it is advised that students take a short break. The Culminating Activity should then be completed over a 3-5 day period. It is recommended that the activity be assigned a score based on completion rather than a rubric.

Stage your own dramatic production. Choose one of the three plays discussed in this Unit:

Trifles by Susan Glaspell
The Boor by Anton Chekov
While the Auto Waits by O. Henry

Choose to stage either the entire play or only a portion of the play. You may perform your production in front of a live audience, film your performance, or do both!

1. Pre-Production

Analyze your play of choice. Reread it and ask yourself, "What will I need to perform this drama?"

Make a few lists:

PROPS—What small, moveable objects will you need in order to perform this play?

SET—What does the environment need to be? Do you need any furniture? Is the play indoors or outdoors? What kinds of entrances and exits do you need?

CAST—How many actors do you need? How many men and how many women?

WARDROBE—What do the characters need to wear? How can the characters' clothes help communicate their personalities?

Culminating Activity

Using the lists that you created, gather and construct everything you will need to perform the drama.

PROPS
Gather the props you will need. Organize them so you know what props are used for what purpose.

SET
Choose a space in which to perform and construct/arrange your set. Try to accurately represent the environment present in your play of choice.

Remember, sets do not always have to be perfect representations of the play's environment. Sometimes, a few elements can suggest the environment, and those suggestions are all the audience needs in order to appreciate the story.

As you construct/arrange your set, remember:
- actors will need to move about the space
- an audience/camera will need to view the entire set
- large objects or walls should not obstruct the view
- the actors will need to come on and go off the set in prearranged entrances and exits

CAST
Contact friends or family members you think will be good choices to portray certain characters. Keep in mind:
- Through costuming, sometimes a man can play a woman's part, or a woman could play a man's part.
- Sometimes, one actor can play multiple parts (as long as the parts are not onstage at the same time).
- Sometimes multiple characters in a play can be combined into one character if not enough actors can be found.

WARDROBE
Gather your costumes. Remember that costuming can tell the audience a lot about a character and setting. Is the setting supposed to be cold? Have the characters wear coats. Is one character supposed to be rich? Have them wear clothes that communicate their wealth to the audience.

D Culminating Activity

2. Rehearsal

Arrange a time to practice with your cast. Rehearse the play a few times and discover how you can best tell the story.

1. Run your lines:

   - Provide a copy of the script for each of your actors.
   - Sit at a table and read from the script. Become familiar with the words. Try to find out which emotions should be communicated through certain words.

> **DIRECTING TIP**
> You are the director of this production. Graciously tell your actors how they can perform to best portray the play. When should they stand? When should they sit? How should they move? How should they deliver their lines? Where should they look? Consider these things and share your vision with your cast. Remember to consider their suggestions as well!

2. Rehearse with actions and props:

   - Once you are comfortable with the lines, go through the play again. This time, deliver your lines coupled with actions, using whatever props are necessary, and interacting with the other actors in a set space.
   - Pay attention to the actions specified in the script, but do not do *only* these actions. The audience needs to be visually engaged throughout the entire play, so the actors cannot only be standing in one place or sitting still for the entire play. Include action throughout the play.

3. Rehearse on set:

   - Practice performing within the set space you predetermined.
   - Interact with the set in the way you think best.
   - Try to never turn your back on the audience! They need to see faces to connect with the characters. Turning the body to face the audience is called *cheating out*.

> **ACTING TIP**
> Imagine that you are your character, not just someone reading words off a page. Imagine the character is real. Do not just deliver lines; couple words with actions—shaking your head, fidgeting, moving around, and so on. Also, imagine what emotions the character is feeling while they speak. Fear? Anger? Curiosity? Try to communicate those emotions in how you deliver the lines.

Culminating Activity

3. Performance

Time to share all your hard work with an audience! Set up a space for an audience to view the production. Make sure that the audience's seats can see everything they need to see on "stage."

If you are filming your performance, make sure that the scope of the camera captures the full extent of the stage.

> You may even use tape on the floor to signify when actors will move out of the scope of the camera. This way, the actors will know to stay within the lines while they are "onstage" and to cross over the lines when they go "offstage."

Deliver your lines with confidence! Make sure the audience can hear you. Always speak up! This is called *projecting*.

> Even if your character "whispers," it cannot be a real whisper, for the audience must hear what is being said. You must "fake whisper" or "stage whisper."

Have fun!

If you wish to share your recorded performance with the team at Essentials in Writing, contact our curriculum team at info@essentialsinwriting.com for uploading instructions!

DRAMA   87

Novel Unit

The Literature You'll Read:

Harper Lee   To Kill a Mockingbird

The Concepts You'll Study:

Analyzing Literature
Protagonist/Antagonist
Setting
External Conflict
Irony
Mood
Symbolism
Theme

Reading Focus
Making Connections
Monitor
Cause and Effect
Making Predictions
Making Inferences
Author's Purpose

Vocabulary
Denotative Meanings

To Kill a Mockingbird

Day 1

WHAT TO LEARN?
- Meet the Author
- Access the Backdrop

Why can't we all just get along?

Women did not always have the same rights as men. In the 1930s South, women were required to adhere to very strict expectations and limitations. Women were expected to dress and behave a certain way while being denied the right to vote, the right to serve on a jury, and access to certain careers.

Men were considered "breadwinners" while women had roles that centered around maintaining the home. While society viewed their roles as inferior, women actually played a vital part in holding their families together and finding ways to survive during the Great Depression.

American Literature

Keep an Eye Out
As you read, keep in mind that women were expected to fulfill certain roles in their homes and families. See if you can identify what those roles were and how women fulfilled or did not fulfill them.

Meet the Author — Nelle Harper Lee

Write About What You Know

In 1960, Nelle Harper Lee wrote the award-winning novel *To Kill a Mockingbird*. Although her story is fiction, the main character, Scout, is not unlike the young Harper Lee. Lee grew up in the small town of Monroeville, Alabama. Her father, a lawyer, was a member of the Alabama state legislature, and her mother suffered from an illness that made it difficult for her to leave the house.

Childhood Friends

Considered a tomboy, Lee protected her childhood friend Truman Capote, who was often picked on for the way he dressed as well as his lack of common interests with other boys his age. Lee would go on the help an adult Capote write an article for The New Yorker which would later become the controversial novel *In Cold Blood*. Lee's childhood gave her an intimate understanding of both the kindness and cruelty of 1930s Southern life which she so vividly and perfectly captured in *To Kill a Mockingbird*.

Apr. 28, 1926–Feb. 19, 2016

NOVEL 89

  Day 2

TO KILL A MOCKINGBIRD

Access the Backdrop

The Southern United States went through a difficult time in the 1930s. Racial tensions were high, and the economy spiraled into depression. Despite the harsh social and economic conditions, Southerners managed to maintain their way of life through hard work and intuition.

> **Keep an Eye Out**
> As you read, keep in mind the strenuous relationship between white people and black people at the time of the story. Because it was commonplace and even taught that black people were lesser, you will notice that many of the characters see nothing wrong with the terrible way that black people are treated. These mindsets are displayed in their words and actions.

The Great Depression

The Great Depression was an unprecedented blow to the American economy that shook the 1930s and defined the decade, leaving nearly one quarter of all working Americans unemployed. The Great Depression was particularly devastating to Southern farmers. People were often forced to barter their possessions in exchange for goods or services.

Racism in the South

Black people were treated as second-class citizens during this time period. **Jim Crow Laws** were state and local regulations that enforced segregation in the South. These statutes suggested that African Americans should be "separate but equal." However, these laws consistently led to inferior African-American schools, transportation, restrooms, and hospitals. Additionally, they dictated the way black people were legally treated, and they reflected the negative attitudes generally held at the time.

 **Day 3**

Section One

Section One: Chapters 1-6 of *To Kill a Mockingbird*

Maycomb is very different place than many twenty-first century cities in the United States. Harper Lee captures colorful characters with quirky mannerisms who demonstrate the Southern life of the 1930s, sometimes with humor and sometimes with dark and dreadful accuracy.

WHAT TO LEARN?
• Protagonist and Antagonist
• Setting
• Making Connections

As you travel back in time with *To Kill a Mockingbird*, remember that because this is an accurate account of what Southern life was like, certain racial slurs or derogatory terms will be used in the same way that they were used historically. This kind of behavior is in no way condoned today, nor was it condoned by Harper Lee; however, it does serve to display the terrible racism that was part of everyday life during the time period in which *To Kill a Mockingbird* is set.

As you read Section One, keep an eye out for answers to the following questions:

What parallels do you see between the childhood of main character Scout and the author's childhood?

What differences are there between the day-to-day life of Maycomb and where you live?

Do you think Harper Lee intentionally included details in the story that were similar to her real-life experiences?

Reading Focus: making connections

As you begin reading *To Kill a Mockingbird*, see if you can **connect** with any of the characters. Are they experiencing an event that is familiar? Do you agree with their beliefs or actions?

You may find connecting to characters in a time so removed from your own difficult. If you are having trouble, try focusing on more general experiences and feelings and avoid specificity.

Reading Focus activity provided in the Resource Book on page 91.

Read Section One (Chapters 1-6) of *To Kill a Mockingbird*

Analyzing Literature — Protagonist and Antagonist

A **character** is any person, creature, or being present in a literary work. Characters have different traits and motives that make them who they are. Stories can have an array of different characters, although specific characters often stand out above the rest.

A **protagonist** is a main character who is usually a hero or heroine and is a key tool used in the development of a story. For this reason, the story revolves around the protagonist as it progresses. A good protagonist often experiences some sort of growth or development as conflict builds in the story.

An **antagonist** is in direct opposition to the protagonist. The antagonist of a story is usually a villain and struggles against the protagonist, creating conflict within the plot.

Choose the character from Section One who is the protagonist. Provide evidence from the text to support your answer.

Who do you think is the antagonist at this point in the story?

Character

Excerpt from the story that supports your answer	Explanation in your own words

Analyzing Literature activity provided in the Resource Book on page 92.

Vocabulary

Look up each word using either a dictionary or the internet and define each word.

chattel
impotent
taciturn
tyrannical
concede
foray
compel
erratic
arbitrate
amiable
ramshackle

 **Day 5**

Analyzing Literature — Setting

The *setting* of a story includes the time and place in which it occurs. This can include weather, historical period, geography, or other features regarding the immediate surrounding. The setting often lends more to a story than a simply creating a backdrop by impacting the story directly in a number of ways.

The setting can influence the *conflict* of a story. For instance, if a ship were trying to cross the ocean, conflict would be worsened by the swift arrival of a tropical storm.

Additionally, the setting of a story can affect the *mood*. For example, if the setting of a story is a dilapidated old house in the middle of a dense forest, isolated from society, the mood of the story would be considered lonely or empty.

What is the setting of *To Kill a Mockingbird*? Be sure to include examples from the text.

Location

Time (Season, Year)

How does the setting influence the characters?

Evidence

Analyzing Literature activity provided in the Resource Book on page 94.

DIVE DEEPER

1. **Analyze** – Contrast Miss Maudie's description of Boo Radley with the folklore recited by Scout shortly after she meets Dill.

2. **Comprehend** – Atticus gives Scout advice that effectively shapes her growth for the rest of the story. He tells her, *"If you can learn a simple trick, Scout, you'll get along a lot better with all kinds of folks. You'll never really understand a person until you consider things from his point of view."* At first, Scout does not understand what Atticus means. Rephrase Atticus' advice in a way that someone Scout's age could easily understand. Then, explain what Atticus meant.

> *Foreshadowing* is the warning or implication of future events.
>
> Several students are introduced when Scout attends school under Miss Caroline, the new teacher. They behave in peculiar ways that confuse the new teacher.
>
> What event might this behavior *foreshadow*? Discuss your answer with your teacher or fellow students.

NOVEL

 Day 6

Check Comprehension

1. **Who** is Miss Caroline Fisher?

2. In the story, Dill challenged Jem's honor by accusing him of being scared. **What** did this accusation prompt Jem to do?

3. **How** does Scout describe Mrs. Dubose?

Think Critically

As the children's curiosity about Boo Radley grows, they elect to create a dramatization "woven from bits and scraps of gossip and neighborhood legend." Most of the scenes the children come up with are glamorized and embellished, such as Mrs. Radley losing all of her hair, teeth, and right forefinger as a result of marrying Mr. Radley and having been bitten by Boo.

While these ideas were mostly in fun and not meant to cause any real harm, they could have hurt the Radleys if someone had witnessed the plays being performed. While mostly fiction, the ideas might have had another effect, this time on the children themselves.

How might the plays that the children created actually have influenced their views of the Radley family? Did they actually start to believe the fiction they had created, or did they remain unaffected? Explain your answer using evidence from the text.

What Happened?

Put the following events that occurred in Section One in the correct, chronological order.

Scout meets Dill Harris.	Miss Caroline Fisher is introduced as Scout's new teacher.
Atticus explains that the Ewells will never change their ways.	The children invent a new game in which they act out the Radleys' lives.
Scout discusses Boo Radley with Miss Maudie on her porch.	Scout, Jem, and Dill sneak onto the Radley's property, and Jem loses his pants.

94   TO KILL A MOCKINGBIRD

 **Day 7**

Section Two

Section Two: Chapters 7-11 of *To Kill a Mockingbird*

WHAT	TO LEARN?
• Conflict (External)	
• Conflict (PVP)	
• Monitor	

The Finch children have many interesting experiences as they grow up in the town of Maycomb. Though the town is small and somewhat unexciting, the children always find ways to make their own excitement, even if that means creating their own fanciful version of reality.

The Finch children latch onto the mystery surrounding Boo Radley, a recluse about whom little is known other than dark rumors. The children imagine a story to explain Boo's absence, which then begins to influence what they really believe about his whereabouts.

Have you ever formed an opinion about someone before you got to know them?

As you read Section Two, keep an eye out for answers to the following questions:

> At the beginning of chapter 7, Scout leaves Jem alone because she "tried to climb into his skin and walk around in it." How do you think she would have behaved differently had she not heeded Atticus' prior advice about empathy?

> Have you ever formed an opinion about someone before you got to know them? How did your opinion change when you actually met the person?

Reading Focus: monitor

As you read Section Two, you will come across different kinds of events. Some events will propel the conflict forward as they make an impact on the plot while others are simply self-contained and may serve no other purpose than further illustrating the experience of the characters. It is important to be able to distinguish the significance of events as the story moves forward.

Reading Focus activity provided in the Resource Book on page 96.

Read Section Two (Chapters 7-11) of *To Kill a Mockingbird*

Day 8

Analyzing Literature — Conflict (External)

Conflict is the struggle between opposing forces. In literature, conflict is intertwined with plot. Characters involved in a story seek to either resolve or avoid the conflict, and their actions in doing so propel the plot forward. Literature contains two major categories of conflict: **external conflict** and **internal conflict.**

External conflict occurs between the protagonist and an **outside** force. Typically, this outside force takes the form of an antagonist; however, there are several other types of external conflict.

External Conflict	
Person vs. Person	Person vs. Nature
Person vs. Society	

In **person vs. person**, a character struggles against another human being, like a thief, an enemy soldier, or a sibling. In **person vs. nature**, a character struggles against some kind of natural phenomenon, like a storm, a dense forest, or animals. In **person vs. society**, a character struggles with an intangible element of their culture, such as poverty, racism, or unfair laws.

Categorize the following examples of external conflict. Then, explain why you chose the category.

1. *"Beautiful my hind foot! If it freezes tonight it'll carry off all my azaleas!"* At this point in the story, Miss Maudie calls Jem over in a panic as she fights to save her flowers.

person vs.	
	Explanation

Analyzing Literature activity provided in the Resource Book on page 98.

Vocabulary

Look up each word using either a dictionary or the internet and define each word.

assure
verge
unfathomable
seldom
caricature
quell
shambles
fanatical
gallantly
vehemently
abide
accustom

Day 9

Analyzing Literature — Conflict (PVP)

Conflict is the struggle between opposing forces. Characters are often thrust into difficult situations in which the opposing force is another person. This kind of opposition is known as **person vs. person conflict**.

In person vs. person conflict, an antagonist becomes an obstacle in the way of the protagonist's progress. This obstruction can be direct, as in a gunfight or a physical battle, or more subtle if another character's views differ from the views of the protagonist, causing them to enter a battle of wits or some other nonphysical impasse.

External Conflict
Person vs. Person

Record examples of person vs. person conflict in this section and explain why the conflict is classified as person vs. person.

Example
Explanation

Analyzing Literature activity provided in the Resource Book on page 100.

DIVE DEEPER

1. **Apply** – Scout gets into a fight with Francis after which she is scolded by Uncle Jack, who misunderstands the situation. Organize the events surrounding Uncle Jack's misunderstanding of Scout's behavior and his realization of what really happened. Which event led to Uncle Jack realizing he was wrong?

2. **Analyze** – Why do you think Uncle Jack chose to keep his promise to Scout and not tell Atticus what really happened? What solution would you have implemented, had you been in Uncle Jack's place? Why?

SYMBOLISM

Symbolism is the use of symbols to convey a deeper or hidden meaning.

What **symbol** is present in the second section of *To Kill a Mockingbird*? What might it represent?

 Day 10

Check Comprehension

1. When Jem, Scout, and Dill build a snowman, **who** was it meant to represent?

2. **What** do the Finch children discover about their father when the mad dog Tim Johnson comes into town? How?

3. **What** is Jem's punishment for executing Mrs. Dubose's camellias?

Think Critically

After a slanderous statement from Mrs. Dubose about Atticus, Jem reacts by losing his temper. When Atticus returns home, he demands that Jem make amends for his wrongdoing.

Scout accompanies Jem as he begins his sentence, which Mrs. Dubose allows. Scout recalls being horrified by Mrs. Dubose's appearance and "fits." The children soon discover that something is seriously wrong with Mrs. Dubose, and Atticus informs them that she is very sick.

Mrs. Dubose dies soon after Jem finishes his sentence, and Atticus informs the children that she had been in immense pain until the day she died. Atticus states that she was a "great lady," to which Jem protests.

Atticus then makes a profound statement. *"She was. She had her own views about things, a lot different from mine, maybe...son, I told you that if you hadn't lost your head I'd have made you go read to her. I wanted you to see something about her–I wanted you to see what real courage is, instead of getting the idea that courage is a man with a gun in his hand. It's when you know you're licked before you begin but you begin anyway and you see it through no matter what. You rarely win, but sometimes you do. Mrs. Dubose won, all ninety-eight pounds of her. According to her views, she died beholden to nothing and nobody. She was the bravest person I ever knew."*

Given Atticus' definition of real courage, do you think that Mrs. Dubose was courageous? Why or why not?

How would you define real courage?

Discussion

Can you think of someone you know that has displayed real courage?

Day 11

Section Three

Section Three: Chapters 12-16 of *To Kill a Mockingbird*

WHAT TO LEARN?
- Situational Irony
- Cause and Effect

Scout and Jem continue with their daily lives, unaware of the severity of what is about to take place. They begin to learn more about the world they live in and start to realize that Maycomb is much darker than they originally imagined.

Aunt Alexandria comes to live with the family, and the trial that Atticus has been ridiculed for draws nearer. The children soon learn that the implications of merely participating in the trial reach far beyond the courtroom.

Have you ever come to the realization that something is not as pleasant as you once imagined it?

As you read Section Three, keep an eye out for the following questions:

> Are more people *for* or *against* Atticus' participation in the trial?

> What is your initial impression of Mr. Dolphus Raymond?

Reading Focus: cause and effect

As you read Section Three, you will come across different kinds of events. Some of the events are catalysts for change and create forward momentum in the story. The events that make these changes and the changes themselves are known as **cause and effect.**

Record the cause of the event listed and then provide evidence from the text to support your answer.

Event
▼
What caused this event?

Reading Focus activity provided in the Resource Book on page 102.

Read Section Three (Chapters 12-16) of *To Kill a Mockingbird*

Analyzing Literature — Situational Irony

Situational irony occurs in literature when the expected outcome of a situation is different than the actual outcome. Often, information is introduced in a story that leads the reader or the characters to expect a certain conclusion. If what actually happens is different than what was expected, the result is known as situational irony.

Identifying ironic events helps the reader make distinctions between expectations and reality.

For example, in *The Wonderful Wizard of Oz*, a certain lion, tinman, scarecrow, and girl embark on a quest to find an ancient wizard who can solve their problems. When they finally reach him, they discover that he is simply a man hiding behind a curtain who is pretending to be an almighty wizard. The audience expects the wizard to be who the main characters seek, but when he turns out to be a fraud, the outcome is different than the expectation and thus qualifies as *situational irony*.

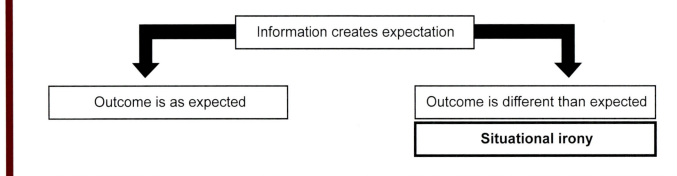

Analyzing Literature: No written activity

Vocabulary

Look up each word using either a dictionary or the internet and define each word.

- altercation
- indignantly
- austere
- dispelled
- formidable
- prerogative
- myopic
- inflection
- elusive
- pensive
- taut
- succinct

Day 13

Analyzing Literature — Situational Irony

Situational irony occurs in literature when the expected outcome of a situation is different than the actual outcome. Often, information is introduced in a story that leads the reader or the characters to expect a certain conclusion. If what actually happens is different than what was expected, the result is known as situational irony.

Identifying ironic events helps the reader make distinctions between expectations and reality.

Record what you expected to happen following the excerpt below. Then, record what actually happened.

Background Information/Events
The children sneak out and find Atticus sitting alone in front of the Maycomb jail. Soon, a large group of men arrive in cars and approach Atticus, staying out of the light. They demand for Atticus to turn Tom Robinson over and inform him that they sent the sheriff out into the woods on a misinformed chase.

Situational Irony

Outcome You Expected

Actual Outcome

Analyzing Literature activity provided in the Resource Book on page 104.

DIVE DEEPER

1. **Know** – Motive is someone's reason for taking action. What is Aunt Alexandria's motivation for coming to live in the Finch household? How do you know?

2. **Analyze** – What conclusion can you draw from the following excerpt?

"–don't see why you touched it in the first place," Mr. Link Deas was saying. "You've got everything to lose from this, Atticus. I mean everything."

SYMBOLISM

Symbolism is the use of symbols to convey a deeper or hidden meaning.

Is a **symbol** present in the third section of *To Kill a Mockingbird*? If so, what might it represent?

Check Comprehension

1. **Why** was Dill hiding under Scout's bed?

2. **Describe** the appearance of First Purchase African M.E. Church.

3. **Who** is Mr. Dolphus Raymond?

Think Critically

Late one night, Jem decides to check on Atticus because he has a "bad feeling." Scout convinces him to let her tag along, and the pair soon becomes a trio when Dill is recruited to join in the adventure.

They find Atticus propped up against the Maycomb county jail, reading. Before giving into the urge to go to him, the children are surprised by the arrival of several strange men who arrive in cars.

The men surround Atticus and seem to be demanding something, referring to Tom Robinson. Jem runs to join his father and refuses to leave his side when Atticus urges him to return home. Scout follows and innocently begins talking to Mr. Cunningham about his son and legal affairs. Her innocence soon appears to soften Mr. Cunningham's cold disposition, and he replies to Scout's request to tell his son "hello" for her.

> "I'll tell him you said hey, little lady," he said.
> Then, he straightened up and waved a big paw. "Let's clear out," he called. "Let's get going, boys."
> As they had come, in ones and twos the men shuffled back to their ramshackle cars. Doors slammed, engines coughed, and they were gone.

1. What do you think would have happened if Scout had not shown up when she did?

2. What would you have done, had you been in Scout's position, to convince the angry mob to leave?

Discussion

Research the term "mob mentality." How does such a term apply to this situation?

Section Four

WHAT TO LEARN?
- Mood
- Making Predictions

Section Four: Chapters 17-21 of *To Kill a Mockingbird*

The trial finally arrives. Tensions run high as Scout and Jem take their seats and survey those in the courthouse. Nearly the whole of Mayberry is in attendance as the trial commences. It is soon revealed that the Ewells are up against Tom Robinson in a case that will shake the town as well as all those involved.

Atticus argues his defense masterfully. By the end of the trial, Jem is convinced that Atticus has won as the jury exits for deliberation.

Do you think Atticus' defense will be enough to sway the jury?

As you read Section Four, keep an eye out for answers to the following questions:

> How do you think the trial would have turned out had it occurred today?

> How has your opinion of Mr. Dolphus Raymond changed?

Reading Focus: making predictions

As you read Section Four, there will be many opportunities for you to **predict** what the outcome of a certain series of events will be. Without knowing it, you use knowledge that you have gathered from the story along with your own experience to predict what might happen next. Making predictions will help you engage with the story because you must pay close attention in order to guess what will happen next.

Record your prediction for the outcome of the trial and then record why you predicted what you did.

Reading Focus activity provided in the Resource Book on page 106.

Read Section Four (Chapters 17-21) of *To Kill a Mockingbird*

Analyzing Literature

Mood

The **mood** of a work of fiction is the prevalent emotion that a reader feels while reading the story. This is typically referred to as the atmosphere of a story or the emotional surroundings. In essence, mood is the feelings that words or descriptions evoke.

Literature can have a depressing mood, a cheerful mood, a suspenseful mood, a frightening mood, or any number of adjectives. It all depends on how the events, surroundings, and atmosphere are described.

Key words can help indicate mood. In the following description, the mood might be considered happy or joyous.

The crowd cheered as the returning soldiers paraded through the streets. Sergeant Smith ran from the march to embrace his wife as tears of joy streamed down his face.

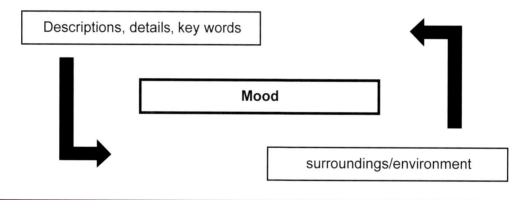

Analyzing Literature: No written activity

Vocabulary

Look up each word using either a dictionary or the internet and define each word.

deigned	acrimonious	tedious	volition
expunge	temerity	aridity	relent
demur	complacently	exodus	perpetrated

 **Day 17**

Analyzing Literature — Mood

The *mood* of a work of fiction is the prevalent emotion that a reader feels while reading the story. This is typically referred to as the atmosphere of a story or the emotional surroundings. In essence, mood is the feelings that words or descriptions evoke.

Literature can have a depressing mood, a cheerful mood, a suspenseful mood, a frightening mood, or any number of adjectives. It all depends on how the events, surroundings, and atmosphere are described.

Record what you think the mood is at different points of the trial based on evidence from the story.

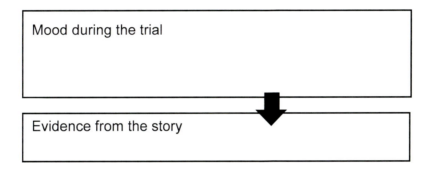

Analyzing Literature activity provided in the Resource Book on page 108.

DIVE DEEPER

1. **Comprehend** – Describe Bob Ewell's relationship with his daughter Mayella using details revealed during the court case as support.

2. **Apply** – Simplify Atticus' argument in the defense of Tom Robinson.

3. **Analyze** – Who do you think is guilty? Draw a conclusion based on all of the evidence presented in the trial.

SYMBOLISM

Symbolism is the use of symbols to convey a deeper or hidden meaning.

Is a **symbol** present in the fourth section of *To Kill a Mockingbird*? If so, what might it represent?

 Day 18

Check Comprehension

1. *How* does Mayella react to being called "ma'am" by Atticus?

2. *Why* does Dill get sick?

3. *What* do the children learn about Mr. Dolphus Raymond?

Think Critically

The wait for the jury to finish their deliberation is long, and the whole of Mayberry sits in quiet anticipation.

The jury finally returns with a verdict, and everyone listens eagerly for the outcome of the trial.

What happened after that had a dreamlike quality; in a dream I saw the jury return, moving like underwater swimmers and Judge Taylor's voice came from far away and was tiny. I saw something only a lawyer's child could be expected to see, could be expected to watch for, and it was like watching Atticus walk into the street, raise a rifle to his shoulder and pull the trigger, but watching all the time knowing the gun was empty.

   A jury never looks at a defendant it has convicted, and when this jury came in, not one of them looked at Tom Robinson. The foreman handed a piece of paper to Mr. Tate who handed it to the clerk who handed it to the judge....
   I shut my eyes. Judge Taylor was polling the jury.
"Guilty...guilty...guilty...guilty..." I peeked at Jem: his hands were white from gripping the balcony rail, and his shoulders jerked as if each "guilty" was a separate stab between them.

1. Did you expect for Tom to be found guilty? How did you feel when he was found guilty?

2. Why do you think Jem was so upset about the outcome of the trial?

Discussion

Why do you think the jury found Tom guilty despite the overwhelming evidence to the contrary?

What do you think will happen to Tom Robinson now?

Day 19

Section Five

Section Five: Chapters 22-26 of *To Kill a Mockingbird*

WHAT TO LEARN?
- Symbolism
- Making Inferences

The trial has finally ended, and the children return home disheartened. They do not understand how Tom Robinson has been found guilty in spite of the evidence presented at the trial.

Many of the town's black residents are grateful for Atticus' noble involvement in the case and shower him with gifts. However, not all members of the town share this opinion. It is soon revealed that Bob Ewell has threatened Atticus and spat in his face, a gesture foreboding the danger that may follow Atticus' defense of Tom Robinson.

Has the danger passed, or has it merely begun?

As you read Section Five, keep an eye out for answers to the following questions:

> Are the Finches in danger?

> Who is on the Finches' side? Who is against them?

Reading Focus: making inferences

When information is left unsaid, an **inference** will help you fill in the gaps. Often in stories, an author will leave out bits and pieces of information so that the audience must come to their own conclusion based on the surrounding context.

The man shut the car door and walked into the house. The drive home had been uneventful, as always.

In the example, the reader may assume that the man got out of his car (even though it is not explicitly stated) based on the surrounding evidence.

Record inferences that you can make from excerpts in Section Five.
Reading Focus activity provided in the Resource Book on page 110.

Read Section Five (Chapters 22-26) of *To Kill a Mockingbird*

NOVEL 107

Analyzing Literature — Symbolism

Symbolism is attaching a deeper meaning to an object or action.

SYMBOL ⟶ Object or action to which deeper meaning is attached

For example, on its own, the color red is very simplistic and may be the color of someone's shirt or a wall. However, depending on the context of a story, red can become a symbol that represents anger or passion.

In the same vein, a handshake on its own is a simple greeting. When used as a symbol, however, it can become a symbol of a union or the solidification of a deal or promise.

Symbolism is a very useful technique in literature to represent something intangible in a way easily understood by an audience. Common symbols include:

Colors: Colors often represent emotions or states of being.

Water: Water is used frequently in literature. It can mean anything from purification to death. If an author specifically mentions an element of water it is usually some form of symbolism.

Darkness: Darkness can represent evil, hiding, and deceit.

Analyzing Literature: No written activity

Vocabulary

Look up each word using either a dictionary or the internet and define each word.

- impertinence
- ruefully
- sibilant
- undue
- acquittal
- vehement
- spurious
- vocation

Day 21

Analyzing Literature — Symbolism

Symbolism is attaching a deeper meaning to an object or action.

SYMBOL ⟶ Object or action to which deeper meaning is attached

Record the symbolism used in Mr. Underwood's editorial. Then, answer the following questions.

- What in the editorial has symbolic significance?
- What does the symbolism mean?
- What did Atticus say that was similar to Mr. Underwood's editorial?

Analyzing Literature activity provided in the Resource Book on page 112.

DIVE DEEPER

1. **Evaluate** – Aunt Alexandra hosts the missionary circle. Their discussion reveals clear contradictions between what they say and what they mean. Determine what the ladies say that is hypocritical or contradictory and explain how it is hypocritical.

2. **Evaluate** – After finding out that his children attended the trial of Tom Robinson, Atticus allows them to stay at the courthouse. Defend Atticus' decision to let Jem attend the trial.

NOVEL 109

 Day 22

Check Comprehension

1. *How* does Atticus respond when Bob Ewell threatens him and spits in his face?

2. At the end of the section, Scout asks Jem a question about their school. *What* is the question, and how does Jem respond?

3. *What* happens to Tom Robinson?

Think Critically

The town was interested in Tom Robinson's death for "maybe two days" but not any longer. Many of the townspeople made derogatory statements, such as claiming that Tom's running was typical behavior for a black person. No one, however, showed much real concern that he had been killed.

Mr. B. B. Underwood, however, had a different opinion that he expressed in the *The Maycomb Tribune*:

Mr. Underwood didn't talk about miscarriages of justice, he was writing so that children could understand. Mr. Underwood simply figured it was a sin to kill cripples, be they standing, sitting, or escaping. He likened Tom's death to the senseless slaughter of songbirds by hunters and children...

How could this be so, I wondered, as I read Mr. Underwood's editorial. Senseless killing–Tom had been given due process of law to the day of his death; he had been tried openly and convicted by twelve good men and true; my father had fought for him all the way. Then Mr. Underwood's meaning became clear: Atticus had used every tool available to free men to save Tom Robinson, but in the secret courts of men's hearts Atticus had no case. Tom was a dead man the minute Mayella Ewell opened her mouth and screamed.

1. If you had been in Mr. Underwood's position, how would you have described Tom's death so that "children could understand"?

2. What did Mr. Underwood mean by "the secret courts of men's hearts"? Explain your answer.

Discussion

Do you think the statement "Tom was a dead man the minute Mayella Ewell opened her mouth and screamed" is accurate? Why or why not?

Day 23

Section Six

WHAT TO LEARN?
- Theme
- Author's Purpose

Section Six: Chapters 27-31 of *To Kill a Mockingbird*

While the trial of Tom Robinson has faded from the minds of many of Maycomb's residents, it is still fresh in the minds and lives of the Finch family as well as others directly involved.

Judge Taylor hears someone prowling just outside of his home in the middle of the night, and Helen, Tom Robinson's wife, is followed by Bob Ewell as he curses at her from a distance. It seems that Bob still holds a grudge against all of those involved in the trial and has begun to seek vengeance.

What do you think Bob Ewell will do?

As you read Section Six, keep an eye out for answers to the following questions:

Is Bob Ewell merely acting menacing, or does he intend to do something terrible?

Try to "walk in the shoes" of different characters as you read by imagining events from their perspectives.

Reading Focus: author's purpose

The reason for which an author writes is known as **author's purpose**. The different kinds of reasons can usually be grouped into three categories: information, entertainment, persuasion.

Works written to inform contain mostly facts, works written to persuade contain mostly opinions, and works intended to entertain are written purely for the enjoyment of the audience.

Record Harper Lee's purpose for writing *To Kill a Mockingbird*.

Reading Focus activity provided in the Resource Book on page 114.

Read Section Six (Chapters 27-31) of *To Kill a Mockingbird*

 Day 24

Analyzing Literature — Theme

Theme is the underlying meaning or idea of a literary work. A theme is intentionally repeated throughout a work using action, dialogue, and symbolism.

A theme can sometimes be obvious while other times it is subtle and must be closely examined to fully understand. Symbols are sometimes intertwined with theme and are used to help communicate it.

Because theme can be abstract, it is sometimes difficult to find. Other than appearing in a repeated, underlying idea, theme can also be found by looking in the following locations:

- The title of a story
- A character's thoughts, actions, and speech
- How a story's conflict is resolved
- The lesson a character learns

Analyzing Literature: No written activity

Vocabulary

Look up each word using either a dictionary or the internet and define each word.

- notoriety
- florid
- nondescript
- eccentricities
- staccato
- reprimand
- bland
- carcass
- repertoire

Day 25

Analyzing Literature — Theme

> *Theme* is the underlying meaning or idea of a literary work. A theme is intentionally repeated throughout a work using action, dialogue, and symbolism.
>
> A theme can sometimes be obvious while other times it is subtle and must be closely examined to fully understand. Symbols are sometimes intertwined with theme and are used to help communicate it.
>
> The tools below can help you discern a story's theme if it is not obvious:
>
> **Close reading**: Can you look more deeply into what is being read? Are there underlying meanings?
> **Repetition**: Is there a particular idea that is continually repeated throughout the work?
> **The Good and the Bad**: What in the story is portrayed as good? What is portrayed as bad?

What is the theme of *To Kill a Mockingbird*?

Theme (one sentence summing the theme)

Clue #1 that pointed toward your answer

Clue #2 that pointed toward your answer

Clue #3 that pointed toward your answer

Analyzing Literature activity provided in the Resource Book on page 116.

DIVE DEEPER

1. Create – After Bob Ewell's vicious attack on the children, we learn that Scout was very nearly cut and that Bob intended to do serious harm to them. Knowing now what took place, recreate the scene as if it had occurred in the day rather than at night. Be sure to include visual descriptions of what took place.

2. Create – Imagine yourself as Scout. After all that has happened, you want to thank Arthur "Boo" Radley for what he did. Write a short thank-you letter to Arthur. Construct your letter properly and choose your words and phrases so that you sound like Scout. Keep in mind her age and personality as you write.

Check Comprehension

1. **What** protects Scout from being cut when Bob Ewell attacks her with a knife?

2. **What** does Heck Tate want to do about Boo Radley killing Bob Ewell?

3. **What** happens to Jem when the children are attacked by Bob Ewell?

Think Critically

After meeting Arthur Radley and escorting him home, Scout is able to finally understand a piece of advice that Atticus offered her long ago.

> *I looked behind me. To the left of the brown door was a long shuttered window. I walked to it, stood in front of it and turned around...Daylight in my mind, the night faded. It was summertime, and two children scampered down the sidewalk toward a man approaching in the distance...*
> *Summertime, and his children played in the front yard with their friend, enacting a strange little drama of their own invention...*
> *It was fall, and his children fought on the sidewalk in front of Mrs. Dubose's. The boy helped his sister to her feet and they made their way home...*
> *Winter, and his children shivered at the front gate, silhouetted against a blazing house. Winter, and a man walked into the street, dropped his glasses, and shot a dog...*
> *Summer, and he watched his children's heart break. Autumn again, and Boo's children needed him.*
> *Atticus was right. One time he said you never really know a man until you stand in his shoes and walk around in them. Just standing on the Radley porch was enough.*

1. Why was Boo Radley so quick to come to Jem and Scout's aid when they were attacked, even though he had never met them in person? Explain your answer.

2. What do you think Scout meant when she said, "Just standing on the Radley porch was enough"? Why was it enough?

Discussion

Can you think of a time when you walked in someone else's shoes? How did walking in their shoes change what you thought about them?

Complete Novel Unit Summative Assessment

Novel Summative Assessment is provided in the Resource Book on page 118.

Culminating Activity

To Kill a Mockingbird *by Harper Lee*

Symbolism Project

Symbolism is present throughout the story as Scout begins to lose her innocence and understand the injustice around her.

Think about how the symbolism of the mockingbird was initially revealed and how Harper Lee used it to effectively communicate that it is wrong to kill something or someone who is innocent. In this activity, you will create your own symbolism to express the theme of *To Kill a Mockingbird*.

After completing the Summative Assessment, it is advised that students take a short break. The Culminating Activity should then be completed over a 3-5 day period. It is recommended that the activity be assigned a score based on completion rather than a rubric.

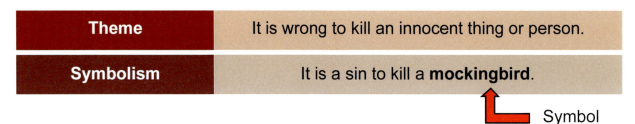

Symbolism is attaching meaning to something that otherwise would have been meaningless, thereby creating a symbol. This usually occurs when an object or action is given a deeper, more significant meaning than exists by simply examining its surface value.

STEP ONE

First, you need to create a **SYMBOL**. It is recommended that the symbol represent *innocence*, much like the mockingbird in the story; however, you may choose to represent something other than *innocence*.

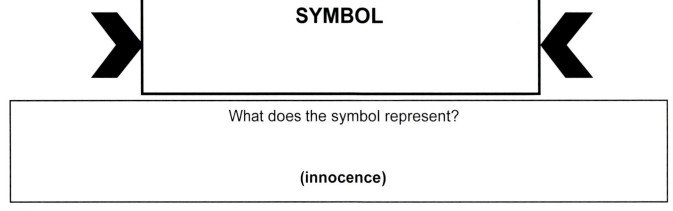

Culminating Activity

To Kill a Mockingbird *by Harper Lee*

Symbolism Project

> Remember: Creating symbolism is a difficult process. It may come naturally, but odds are it will take a little time, and that is fine!

During this step, you will create one sentence to express the symbolism. Remember, your sentence should represent the theme of *To Kill a Mockingbird*:

Theme	It is wrong to kill an innocent thing or person.

For example, if the theme were "protecting freedom is important," the **symbol** might be an eagle and your complete symbolism might be the following: *It is paramount that we preserve the eagle.*

2. Create **one sentence** and include the **symbol** that describes the theme using symbolism.

Theme	It is wrong to kill an innocent thing or person.

Symbolism	

NOVEL 117

Culminating Activity

To Kill a Mockingbird *by Harper Lee*

Symbolism Project

> Almost done! Take a breath, and move on to the final step!

During the final step, you will present your creation in one of three forms. Included in your presentation should be how you came up with the symbolism, its relevance to the theme, and an explanation of the underlying ideas.

FINAL STEP!

 Choose one of the following three methods to present the symbolism you created. Treat your audience like they do not know the meaning behind the symbolism and describe it to them in great detail.

A. Essay

Present the symbolism in a five-paragraph essay. Your essay should include the symbol you created (why you chose it and its relevance to the theme) and the meaning of the symbolism (an explanation of its underlying ideas).

B. Board/Model

Present the symbolism visually. Create a project board or another model to present your creation. You may use images or crafts to assist you in the presentation. Remember to be creative! You must visually represent the symbol you created (why you chose it and its relevance to the theme) and the meaning of the symbolism (an explanation of its underlying ideas).

C. Speech

Write a speech to present the symbolism. Your speech must be no longer than five minutes and must include the symbol you created (why you chose it and its relevance to the theme) and the meaning of the symbolism (an explanation of its underlying ideas).

This page is intentionally blank.

Poetry Unit

The Literature You'll Read:

Billy Collins	Introduction to Poetry
Naoshi Koriyama	A Loaf of Poetry
Alice Walker	Women
Rudyard Kipling	If—
Thomas Hardy	Ah, are you digging on my grave?
John Donne	Go and catch a falling star
Elizabeth Bishop	One Art
Elizabeth Barrett Browning	How Do I Love Thee?
Frank O'Hara	Having a Coke with you
e e cummings	[in Just-]
Gwendolyn Brooks	*We Real Cool
Phillis Wheatley	*On Being Brought from Africa to America
William Wordsworth	*I Wandered Lonely as a Cloud

The Concepts You'll Study:

Analyzing Figurative Language
Metaphor
Simile
Personification
Hyperbole
Symbolism
Allusion

Writing Connection
Poetry with Figurative Language
Fixed Forms
Rhymed Poetry

Element of Poetry
Theme
Voice
Diction
Mood
Rhyme Scheme
Rhythm
Tone
Dialect

*Summative Assessment

 Day 1

Poetry

"Poetry is when an emotion has found its thought and the thought has found words." - Robert Frost

Poetry is a genre of literature that is condensed, intense, shaped, and sparse. Unlike **prose** (short stories, novels, and nonfiction), poetry communicates to the reader with only a few words chosen for their sound, meaning, and impact. This genre can tell a story, offer an image, or express intangible things like feelings or thoughts.

What do POETS say about POETRY?

"Most people ignore most poetry because most poetry ignores most people."
— Adrian Mitchell

"Poetry is truth in its Sunday clothes."
— Joseph Roux

"Poetry is a deal of joy and pain and wonder, with a dash of the dictionary."
— Kahlil Gibran

"Poetry is the journal of a sea animal living on land, wanting to fly in the air."
— Carl Sandburg

"Poetry is eternal graffiti written in the heart of everyone."
— Lawrence Ferlinghetti

"Poetry is ... that time of night, lying in bed, thinking what you really think, making the private world public, that's what the poet does."
— Allen Ginsberg

The value of reading poetry is difficult to explain, for it is something that cannot be quantified. Poetry can help readers consider new concepts or articulate tricky emotions. Poems can take the familiar and present it in a new light, but they can also take the unfamiliar and make it seem like something you knew all along. Some people may feel intimidated by poetry, thinking they cannot understand it. Developing the skills to enjoy poetry takes time and effort, for poems are built upon the use of figurative language and certain literary elements.

RHYTHM AND METER

Poetry is made up of **lines** and **stanzas** (groups of lines). Stanzas can be of any length, but those with specific lengths have special names.

- **a couplet** – *a two-line stanza*
- **a tercet** – *a three-line stanza*
- **a quatrain** – *a four-line stanza*
- **a sestet** – *a six-line stanza*
- **an octave** – *an eight-line stanza*

A poem's **rhythm** is the arrangement of stressed and unstressed syllables. **Stress** is spoken emphasis.

STRESS
power (POW-er) – the first syllable is emphasized
although (al-THOUGH) – the second syllable is emphasized
notebook (NOTE-BOOK) – both syllables are emphasized
poetry (PO-e-try) – the first syllable is emphasized
fantastic (fan-TAS-tic) – the second syllable is emphasized

Some poems have **regular rhythm**, a repeating pattern of stressed and unstressed syllables. Specific patterns of stressed and unstressed syllables are described in **feet**.

VERSE FEET
Iamb: two syllables; unstressed-stressed (/ ^)
Trochee: two syllables; stressed-unstressed (^ /)
Anapest: three syllables; unstressed-unstressed-stressed (/ / ^)
Dactyl: three syllables; stressed-unstressed-unstressed (^ / /)

When poetic lines have a fixed number of feet per line, they have a fixed **meter**.

FEET PER LINE
3 – **Trimeter** ("tri-" means three)
4 – **Tetrameter** ("tetra-" means four)
5 – **Pentameter** ("penta-" means five)
6 – **Hexameter** ("hexa-" means six)

Identifying the pattern of feet and meter in a poem is called **scanning**. When scanning, a (/) is used to indicate an unstressed syllable and a (^) is used to indicate a stressed syllable.

Consider Robert Frost's "Mending Wall":

> / ^ / ^ / ^ / ^ / ^
> Something there is that doesn't love a wall,
> / ^ / ^ / ^ / ^ / ^
> That sends the frozen-ground-swell under it,
> / ^ / ^ / ^ / ^ / ^
> And spills the upper boulders in the sun;
> / ^ / ^ / ^ / ^ / ^
> And makes gaps even two can pass abreast. ...

Robert Frost, ca. 1915

The stress pattern is *unstressed-stressed*, which is an iambic foot. There are five iambs per line, so the meter is pentameter. Therefore, "Mending Wall" is written in *iambic pentameter*.

Sometimes, rhythm can be measured in **beats**, which are based on emphasized words rather than stressed syllables.

When a poem does not utilize a repeating pattern of feet or beats, the poem has **irregular rhythm.**

POETRY 123

SOUND

Sound devices are part of what makes poetry both enjoyable and meaningful. Certain sounds can create particular moods for poetry, such as mournful and serious, energetic and optimistic, or harsh and unpleasant.

Repeated sounds or words lend a poem a pleasing and memorable flow. Words that sound the same **rhyme**. **Internal rhyme** (or **middle rhyme**) occurs within a poetic line, and **end rhyme** occurs at the end of multiple poetic lines.

> What feelings do the sounds of these words evoke?
>
> *ponder, wander, down, lore, slow, mood*
>
> *think, skip, pip, peak, speak, delicious*
>
> *chatter, hatchet, kinetic, tatter, blast, rake*

Sometimes words do not rhyme exactly, but they sound similar enough that poets will use them as if they rhymed. This is called **slant rhyme** (or **approximate rhyme**).

The pattern of rhyme in a poem is referred to as the **rhyme scheme**. A poem's rhyme scheme is annotated using lowercase letters at the ends of the lines. Lines that rhyme are labeled with the same letter, and each new rhyme is labeled with a new letter.

"Flower Gathering" by Robert Frost

I left you in the morning,	a
And in the morning glow	b
You walked a way beside me	c
To make me sad to go.	b
Do you know me in the gloaming,	d
Gaunt and dusty gray with roaming?	d
Are you dumb because you know me not,	e
Or dumb because you know?...	b

> The lines labeled *b* rhyme with each other, and the lines labeled *d* rhyme with each other.
>
> The *a*, *c*, and *e* lines do not rhyme with any other lines, but we still label them with their own letters to indicate the sounds.

The rhyme scheme of this poem would be written out as "abcbddeb."

OTHER SOUND DEVICES

Alliteration – repeated *initial* consonant sounds in close proximity

Assonance – repeated *vowel* sounds in close proximity

Consonance – repeated consonant *sounds* in close proximity that appear anywhere in words (beginning, middle, or end)

 Day 4

FIXED FORMS

Some poems are written according to **fixed forms**, meaning they have a set amount of lines and stanzas and adhere to a specific meter and rhyme scheme.

Sonnet

A sonnet is a poem with fourteen lines, a specific rhyme scheme and meter, and a precise division of thought. This has been a popular poetic form since the 1200s and has many variations, but two major categories take precedence.

An **Italian sonnet** is divided between an octave and a sestet.

RHYME SCHEME
abbaabba cde cde

The *octave* presents an idea or problem, and the *sestet* provides a reply or answer to the octave.

An **English sonnet** is divided between three *quatrains* and a *couplet*.

RHYME SCHEME
abab cdcd efef gg

In the quatrains, an idea or problem is developed with three examples, and the couplet intensifies or answers the three quatrains.

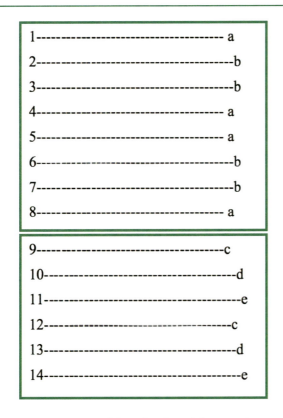

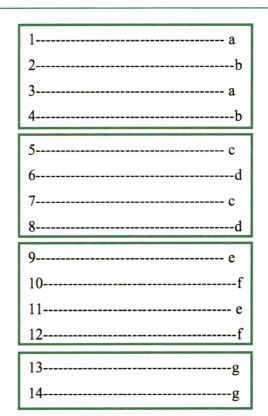

All sonnets are written in *iambic pentameter*, with only occasional discrepancies.

POETRY 125

 Day 4

Villanelle
A villanelle is a poem with nineteen lines separated into five *tercets* and one *quatrain*. This form does not have a fixed meter per line but does require a specific rhyme scheme and repeating pattern.

Repeated lines called **refrains** can be exact or near exact copies.

Free Verse
A free verse is a poem that does not adhere to a specific rhyme or meter. Free verse has become a popular mode of expression in modern times as it is an excellent form to use when expressing personal thoughts, feelings, or experiences.

"When I Heard The Learn'd Astronomer"
by Walt Whitman

When I heard the learn'd astronomer,
When the proofs, the figures, were ranged in columns before me,
When I was shown the charts and diagrams, to add, divide, and measure them,
When I sitting heard the astronomer where he lectured with much applause in the lecture-room,
How soon unaccountable I became tired and sick,
Till rising and gliding out I wander'd off by myself,
In the mystical moist night-air, and from time to time,
Look'd up in perfect silence at the stars.

Villanelle basic form:	
(Refrain #1)	a
(line)	b
(Refrain #2)	a
(line)	a
(line)	b
(Refrain #1)	a
(line)	a
(line)	b
(Refrain #2)	a
(line)	a
(line)	b
(Refrain #1)	a
(line)	a
(line)	b
(Refrain #2)	a
(line)	a
(line)	b
(Refrain #1)	a
(Refrain #2)	a

Ode
a short lyrical poem that is serious in tone and subject matter.

Elegy
a poem of lamentation and mourning that honors someone who has died.

Ballad
a poem that narrates a story, typically with short stanzas, often accompanied by music.

Epic
a twelve-part narrative poem with a heroic main character who goes on a fantastic adventure.

 Day 5

OTHER POETIC ELEMENTS

Theme is the underlying message of a poem or its significance to life.

| **Theme can be revealed in many ways:** | • the title
• repeated elements
• what is portrayed positively or negatively
• the overall point made by the speaker |

MOOD
Mood is how a reader feels in response to a poem. Mood can be dictated by subject matter, word choice, or the resolution of a poem. The mood of a poem can be amusing, depressing, eerie, festive, and so on.

TONE
Tone is how the poet feels about their subject matter, which is communicated through the poem. Tone is not dictated by subject matter but rather how the poet treats the subject matter. Many poets have written about death, but the tones of such poems vary among fearful, anticipatory, resigned, mournful, and indifferent.

VOICE
Voice is the speaker in a poem or the poet's personal style.

Speaker
Sometimes the speaker (or narrator) is the poet, but sometimes a writer will create a poem from a different perspective. A male poet can employ a female speaker, a young female poet can employ an older female speaker, and poets can even employ nonhuman speakers (such as animals, aspects of nature, or abstract concepts like Truth).

Style
Each poet develops their own style (poetic voice). Readers identify a poet's unique style by reading multiple works by the poet. Frequent subject matter, usual tone, and diction help reveal a writer's individual voice.

Diction is the *vocabulary* (word choice) and *syntax* (word order and punctuation) of a poem. Diction can be regular (known words and a recognizable arrangement) or irregular (invented or unusual words in an unorthodox arrangement) as well as formal or informal.

Dialect is a way of speaking that is specific to a geographic location or social group.

POETRY

FIGURATIVE LANGUAGE

Poets employ **figurative language** to make their writing more poignant, persuasive, or pleasing. Figurative language uses words, phrases, and expressions that mean something different or more than their literal interpretation.

Literal language presents facts, but figurative language involves the imagination.

Literal Description: *A tremendous, dark cloud is on the horizon, with thunder warning of the storm's coming.*

Figurative Description: *The cloud sits on the horizon like a tiger ready to pounce, and growls of thunder reverberate, warning of the predator's coming.*

Simile

A simile is an imaginative comparison that uses the word like or as. A simile draws attention to the similarities between two objects, actions, or ideas. By bringing up this comparison, a poet is able to evoke the emotions or images related with one thing and apply them to another.

"Going for Water" by Robert Frost

...*We ran as if to meet the moon*
That slowly dawned behind the trees...

But once within the wood, we paused
Like gnomes that hid us from the moon...

Running (to the water) *as if* running to meet the moon

We (the children) *are like* gnomes

Through use of similes, Frost communicates the freedom and imagination that can accompany children doing simple chores.

Metaphor

A metephor is an imaginative comparison that does not use the word like or as. Metaphors precisely describe an object, action, or idea by equating it with something else. An extended metaphor is a metaphor that continues throughout an entire poem.

"The Silken Tent" by Robert Frost

She is as in a field a silken tent
At midday when a sunny summer breeze
Has dried the dew and all its ropes relent,
So that in guys it gently sways at ease,
And its supporting central cedar pole,
That is its pinnacle to heavenward
And signified the sureness of the soul...

A woman *is* a silken tent

Through use of this metaphor, Frost describes a woman's beauty and strength.

Personification

Personification is giving human traits and emotions to nonhuman or non-living things. It can communicate a particular tone, appearance, or action that is difficult to describe for nonhuman things, and it can also help readers connect with nonhuman elements in poems.

"My November Guest" by Robert Frost

My <u>Sorrow</u>, when she's here with me,
    Thinks these dark days of autumn rain
Are beautiful as days can be;
She loves the bare, the withered tree;
    She walks the sodden pasture lane. ...

> Sorrow is personified
>
> By personifying his sorrow as a human guest, the speaker is able to poetically describe when and where he feels most sorrowful.

Hyperbole

A hyperbole is an extreme exaggeration in order to make a point. Overstatement can emphasize the truth of a statement or concept, and it can be humorous or serious as well as obvious or subtle.

"After Apple-Picking" by Robert Frost

...For I have had too much
Of apple-picking: I am overtired
Of the great harvest I myself desired.
<u>There were ten thousand thousand fruit to touch</u>,
Cherish in hand, lift down, and not let fall. ...

> "Ten thousand thousand" (that is, ten million) apples is an extreme exaggeration of how many apples the speaker picked. The hyperbole communicates how the speaker feels about how many apples he has picked rather than the literal number.

Imagery

Imagery is words and phrases that appeal to the reader's senses, including sight, hearing, taste, smell, and touch. Imagery makes poems become alive and vibrant; it creates a more fulfilling experience than reading dull words on a page.

"Out, Out—" by Robert Frost

"The buzz saw <u>snarled</u> and <u>rattled</u> in the yard
And <u>made dust and dropped stove-length sticks of wood</u>,
<u>Sweet-scented stuff</u> when <u>the breeze drew across it.</u>
And from there those that lifted eyes could count
<u>Five mountain ranges one behind the other</u>
<u>Under the sunset</u> far into Vermont. ...

> This excerpt is full of imagery that appeals to sight, sound, smell, and touch.

Symbolism

Symbolism is the use of a person, place, object, or action to express a deeper or double meaning, sometimes describing an intangible idea or concept.

Symbolism in a poem can be discerned through:
- **immediate context** – Does the poem itself reveal any symbolic meaning?
- **your own reasoning and experience** – Does the poem mention anything that may have multiple layers of meaning based on your own reasoning?
- **knowledge of common symbols** – Does the poem use any commonly recognized symbols? (This knowledge will grow with your exposure to literature.)

"The Road Not Taken" by Robert Frost

*Two roads diverged in a yellow wood,
And sorry I could not travel both
And be one traveler, long I stood
And looked down one as far as I could
To where it bent in the undergrowth; ...*

> Symbol: the roads
> Symbolic meaning: life choices
>
> The narrator of the poem considers the two roads just like someone would consider two choices in life. A *road* or *path* is also a common symbol for life, so coming upon two roads is symbolic for approaching a choice which will affect the direction of one's life.

Allusion

An allusion is a reference to something outside a piece of literature. The reference helps communicate the poet's point or draw connections between two things.

Allusions can reference:
- **history** (Julius Caesar, discovering the Americas, and Omaha Beach)
- **culture or society** (common products such as Coca-Cola, companies such as Ford, and traditions such as fireworks on the Fourth of July)
- **other pieces of art and literature** (*Romeo and Juliet*, the Trojan Horse, and Michelangelo's *David*)

Many allusions in literature reference other pieces of literature. In order to identify and understand allusions, a reader needs a certain knowledge of other works of literature. Therefore, appreciating allusions is something that will come with time and exposure.

"Stars" by Robert Frost

*...And yet with neither love nor hate,
    Those stars like some snow-white
Minerva's snow-white marble eyes
    Without the gift of sight.*

> Allusion: Minerva
>
> Minerva is the Roman equivalent of the Greek goddess Athena. By making this reference, Frost communicates that the stars watch people like the goddess does in mythology. (The "marble" alludes to statues of Athena.)

Introduction to Poetry
A Loaf of Poetry

Day 1: Before You Read

WHAT TO LEARN?
- Metaphor and Simile
- Theme

Just tell me what it MEANS

Many people may think poems are puzzles to be solved or secret messages to be decoded and that the goal in reading poetry is to crack this puzzling code. They may think poets intentionally confuse readers or that poems are written in a weird and mysterious language. While it may sometimes feel this way, this is not an entirely accurate view of poetry.

All poems have meaning, but sometimes the purpose of a poem is to offer pure enjoyment, a respite from the struggles of everyday life. Not every poem has a secret truth about the world that is waiting to be discovered. Other times, a poem does contain a truth birthed from life experiences, but this truth is found through experiencing and dwelling on the poem, not pulling it apart like a detective looking for evidence.

Billy Collins' poem about reading poetry and Naoshi Koriyama's poem about writing poetry demonstrate these points in simple, poignant ways.

Meet the Authors

American Literature

Poet and Teacher

Billy Collins
b. 1941

Collins has written over a dozen books of poetry, most of which is humorous, and has taught English at multiple universities in his home state of New York. Collins has commented that "the mind can be trained to relieve itself on paper" and that "high school is the place where poetry goes to die."

World Literature

Naoshi Koriyama
b. 1926

The Power of Poetry

Born and raised in Japan, Koriyama moved to the U.S. in 1950 to study English and social studies. During this time, he became interested in poetry in order to fight against loneliness. In 1954, he moved back to Japan to teach and write poetry.

POETRY

Day 2: Before You Read

Analyzing Figurative Language — Metaphor and Simile

A *metaphor* is an imaginative comparison between two things or concepts, claiming that one thing is another. An *extended metaphor* is a metaphor that continues throughout an entire poem. Similarly, a *simile* is an imaginative comparison that uses the word like or as. Through metaphors and similes, poets describe similarities between objects, actions, and ideas, thereby creating images in the minds of readers.

Metaphor:	Simile:
Hate *is* a heavy chain.	Joy *is like* sunlight.

Metaphors and similes are not always written in a cut-and-dry format. Sometimes, the comparison is subtler:

> My life chugs along the track,
> passing pretty scenes
> and coughing up smog
> once in a while.

The metaphor: My life is a train.

Identify at least five metaphors or similes in the two poems and explain what the comparisons mean. Also, identify and explain the extended metaphor present in one of the poems. Indicate the poem from which you take each example and mark the comparison you think is the most effective.

Metaphor or Simile	What does it mean?
A poem is a beehive	A poem has a lot of activity going on beneath the surface, and a reader can understand (or "hear") it if they pay attention, just like with a beehive.

Analyzing Figurative Language activity provided in the Resource Book on page 125.

Element of Poetry: Theme

Theme is the underlying message of a poem or its significance to life. A poem's theme can be revealed through the title, repeated elements, what is portrayed positively or negatively, and the overall point made by the speaker.

Summarize the theme of "Introduction to Poetry" by Billy Collins in one sentence. List three pieces of evidence from the text that show how the poem reveals the theme. Evaluate the theme, determining its importance or value.

Theme Sentence here	Evidence Three pieces of evidence from the poem
Evaluation This theme is [important or not important] because...	

Element of Poetry activity provided in the Resource Book on page 126.

Read "Introduction to Poetry" by Billy Collins and "A Loaf of Poetry" by Naoshi Koriyama

 Day 3: After You Read

Think About It

1. In Billy Collins' "Introduction to Poetry," who is "I," and who are "they"? How do you know? (Hint: Look at the title of the poem and consider Collins' personal experience.)

2. In "Introduction to Poetry," what is the difference between how "I" and "they" think about poetry?

3. What do you think the speaker of "Introduction to Poetry" means when he says, "I want them to waterski / across the surface of a poem"?

4. Both "Introduction to Poetry" and "A Loaf of Poetry" offer musings about poems. What is similar or different about the speakers' tones?

Connection Reflection

5. The speaker of "Introduction to Poetry" is very frustrated with other people because they do not understand how to read poetry properly. This is similar to how teachers are sometimes frustrated with their students, but students can be frustrated with their teachers, too. Have you ever been involved in a situation where the leader and the students did not understand each other? What do you think caused this division?

6. In "A Loaf of Poetry," Koriyama likens writing poetry to the comforting but strenuous activity of making bread. To what activity would you liken writing poetry, and why?

After you **read** a poem and **understand** its language, ask yourself, **what does it mean?**

Main Idea

Both "Introduction to Poetry" by Billy Collins and "A Loaf of Poetry" by Naoshi Koriyama are poems about poetry, but they approach the subject from different angles. Collins' poem focuses on reading poetry while Koriyama's poem focuses on writing poetry.

What does "Introduction to Poetry" say about how a poem should be read?

B

What does "A Loaf of Poetry" say about how a poem should be written?

POETRY

 Day 4: After You Read

Writing Connection

There are very few "rules" for writing poetry. Any subject can be turned into a poem, any rhythm and rhyme scheme can be used or ignored, and any number of themes—great and small—can be expressed. The key to writing poetry is being intentional about one's rhythm and word choice and to employ figurative language and poetic elements as they fit in the poem.

Write a poem that means something to you personally—either an expression of your feelings or thoughts or a description of something or someone important to you. Employ a metaphor or simile in your poem to help communicate what you mean.

Breaking Boundaries

Culture Clash – Billy Collins is an American poet while Naoshi Koriyama is a Japanese poet, and Western and Eastern traditions in poetry differ significantly. Research the basic tenets of Western and Eastern poetry and explore their differences.

Words and Pictures – Both "Introduction to Poetry" and "A Loaf of Poetry" are full of sensory imagery. Illustrate one or both of the poems in the way you think best visually represents the content and tone of the poem.

If– / Women

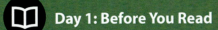
Day 1: Before You Read

WHAT TO LEARN?
- Personification
- Voice and Diction

Where are you going, where have you been?

Life for many people in the twenty-first century is relatively easy and enjoyable. Much of the hardship people's ancestors experienced—such as war, famine, and economic depression—either do not directly affect current generations or do not affect them at all. Quite recently, however, people dealt with both World Wars, shortages of food and jobs, and widespread racism and sexism.

The advantages and privileges many people enjoy today are the result of hard work on behalf of parents, grandparents, and great-grandparents. Being mindful of those who came before us and made this life possible can impact our decisions today.

Do you know any interesting stories about your ancestors? Were they involved in any major events in your state or country? Discuss your answers with your teacher or fellow classmates.

Meet the Authors

British Literature

"The Most Complete Man of Genius"

Rudyard Kipling
Dec 30, 1865–Jan 18, 1936

A Brit who spent most of his life in India, Joseph Rudyard Kipling holds the distinction of being the youngest recipient of the Nobel Prize for Literature at the age of forty-two. He is most famous for *The Jungle Book* and *Just-So Stories*, both heavily influenced by his time in India, which was then colonized by the British. His support of British imperialism in India has made him a controversial figure in recent decades, but the majority of his literature can be enjoyed regardless of his politics.

American Literature

Alice Walker
b. 1944

"I Had to Keep a Lot in My Mind"

Born in Georgia to sharecropper parents, Alice Malsenior Walker grew up under Jim Crow laws and an atmosphere of heavy racism. Her mother fought for her children to receive an education, and Walker began writing literature at the age of eight, eventually graduating as valedictorian of her class and supporting the Civil Rights Movement in college. In 1982, she published *The Color Purple*, her most popular and influential novel. Walker's poems and short stories focus on the struggles of black people, especially black women, in a racist and sexist society.

POETRY

Day 2: Before You Read

Analyzing Figurative Language — Personification

When an author uses **personification**, they are giving human traits and emotions to nonhuman or non-living things. Personification is a popular choice of figurative language in literature because it helps the reader identify abstract concepts and understand them better.

Identify three examples of personification in Kipling's "If—." Then, use each personification in a new context that you create.

Analyzing Figurative Language activity provided in the Resource Book on page 128.

> Personification can help emphasize something to the reader, such as in the poem "Two Sunflowers Move in the Yellow Room" by William Blake:
>
> "Ah, William, we're weary of weather,"
> said the sunflowers, shining with dew.
> "Our traveling habits have tired us.
> Can you give us a room with a view?"
>
> Flowers and other parts of nature do not grow weary and do not travel, but Blake personifies the sunflowers to portray the desire to be somewhere else, even if that place is not where we are meant to be.

Example of Personification in Poem	Personification in New Context
"Ah, William, we're weary of weather," said the sunflowers, shining with dew.	"Ah, William, why are we here?" asked the sunflowers, trapped in the vase.

Element of Poetry: Voice and Diction

In poetry, voice and diction work together to create a poet's individual sound. **Voice** can refer to the *speaker* of a poem or to the poet's personal *style*. The speaker of a poem is not always the writer. The speaker could be an angry man, an old woman, a hungry child, a lonely tree, and so on. The speaker is identified based on evidence in the poem—their emotions, their process of thought, and their tone.

Diction refers to the vocabulary (word choice) and syntax (word order and punctuation) of a poem. It can be presented in a formal or casual manner.

The combination of voice and diction produces a work of literature that displays the unique sound of a poet.

Summarize the voice and diction of Kipling's "If—" and Walker's "Women" in one sentence each. Compare and contrast the voice and diction of the poems and record their similarities and differences. (For this activity, focus only on the speaker aspect of voice.)

Element of Poetry activity provided in the Resource Book on page 130.

Read "If–" by Rudyard Kipling and "Women" by Alice Walker

 Day 3: After You Read

Think About It

1. In "If—", the speaker says it is important to dream and to think but to not "make dreams your master" nor make "thoughts your aim." Do you agree? Why or why not?

2. What do you think the speaker of "If—" means when he says that all men "should count with you, but none too much"? What might "count" mean in this context?

3. What is the relationship between the "we" in Walker's poem and the women Walker describes?

4. What does the speaker of "Women" mean when she says that the women in the poem "knew what we must know"? (Hint: study the surrounding lines of the poem.)

Connection Reflection

5. "If—" is a list of qualities, actions, and mindsets that, according to its speaker, comprise the ideal man or the ideal woman and make him or her the best person they can be. If you were to make a list of what makes someone an ideal man or woman, what would be included in it? Brainstorm at least five criteria and explain your reasoning behind each of your choices.

6. Alice Walker's "Women" describes the women who, through hard work and sacrifice, created possibilities and opportunities for the women who came after them. Is there someone in your life who worked hard in order to give you a better life or who sacrificed something in order to support you? Who is this person, and what did they do for you?

After you **read** a poem and **understand** its language, ask yourself, **what does it mean?**

Main Idea

Both "If—" and "Women" discuss certain qualities that make a person worthy of admiration; however, the subjects of the poem are different. "If—" describes a person in the present, and "Women" describes people in the past.

What is the result of accomplishing all the "ifs" Kipling talks about in his poem? Why is this result desirable?

B

Who are the women in Walker's poem? What is so important about what they did for the "we" in the poem?

Day 4: After You Read

Writing Connection

Personification carries a certain charm with it when used in literature because it gives nonhuman concepts and entities personalities. These personalities help convey the concepts' meaning. Because of this, personification is a popular form of figurative language in children's poetry, but it is also used widely in poetry for older audiences as well.

Write a poem that uses personification to discuss any topic of your choice.

Breaking Boundaries

Researching Rudyard – Did Rudyard Kipling's life reflect the view of manhood he describes in "If—"? In other words, did his personal lifestyle display the virtues and actions he extols in this poem? Research his life and the opinions of his contemporaries to determine your answer.

Visual Verse – The specific and concrete nature of poetry imbues it with the ability to inspire mental pictures in its readers' minds. Draw, sketch, paint, or otherwise visually depict the warlike scene Walker describes in lines 12-18 of "Women."

Ah, Are You Digging on My Grave? Go and Catch a Falling Star

Day 1: Before You Read

WHAT TO LEARN?
- **Hyperbole**
- Mood and Rhyme Scheme

What we have here is a failure to COMMUNICATE

"You're being birddogged, scooch."
"Let's blow up the cheese."
"She's all that and a bag of chips."
"Noob, u just got pwnd."

The way people use language changes, as evidenced by how slang has evolved since the 1950s. The English language has transformed bit by bit for centuries, so sometimes when we read poetry written hundreds of years ago, the language can be tricky to understand. For example, word order in sentences can be different, and some vocabulary can be used that modern readers no longer utilize.

Even with the differences, readers can still understand older poetry if they take the time to work through what the poets are saying, poets such as Thomas Hardy and John Donne.

British Literature

Meet the Authors

British Literature

Where to bury a body...

Thomas Hardy
June 2, 1840–Jan 11, 1928

John Donne
Jan 22, 1573–Mar 31, 1631

That's the power of love

Hardy was a novelist and poet. He achieved literary fame during his lifetime and influenced other writers such as D. H. Lawrence and Virginia Woolf. When he died, there was controversy about where he should be buried. Ultimately, his heart was buried next to his first wife, and his ashes were buried in Poets' Corner of Westminster Abbey in London.

Donne wrote many poems about love before ever meeting his wife, Anne More. The couple had quite a story, complete with a secret marriage, financial destitution, and twelve children. It was during his marriage and after his wife's death that Donne wrote some of his finest poems, known as the Holy Sonnets.

POETRY **139**

 Day 2: Before You Read

Analyzing Figurative Language — Hyperbole

Hyperbole is extreme exaggeration used to make a point. When a poem claims, "The sun does not rise until I see my love," the statement should not be taken literally. Rather, the exaggeration communicates that the speaker's significant other is as important as the sun is to the day. Hyperbole can be humorous or serious as well as subtle or outrageous.

In John Donne's "Go and catch a falling star," the speaker tells his audience (presumably a young man) to do many impossible things. These commands are a form of subtle hyperbole.

Identify three usages of hyperbole in Donne's poem and rewrite them to be more applicable to your own time period and experiences. In one sentence, summarize the hyperbolic message of the entire poem.

Hyperbole in Poem	New Hyperbole
"Go and catch a falling star"	Go keep pace with a 747

Analyzing Figurative Language activity provided in the Resource Book on page 132.

Element of Poetry: Mood and Rhyme Scheme

Mood is how a reader feels in response to a piece of literature. Subject matter and word choice have a major impact on a poem's mood, but **rhyme scheme** also has an effect. Complex, intricate rhyme schemes lend the poem a serious and important mood. In contrast, frequent and simple rhymes create a lighthearted, frivolous impression.

Record the repeating rhyme scheme of Hardy's "Are you digging on my grave?" and explain how the rhyming pattern influences the mood. Rewrite a stanza of the poem according to a different rhyme scheme to observe how it changes the mood.

Element of Poetry activity provided in the Resource Book on page 134.

Read "Ah, Are You Digging on My Grave?" by Thomas Hardy and "Go and Catch a Falling Star" by John Donne

Day 3: After You Read

Think About It

1. In "Are you digging on my grave?", why do you think Hardy wrote from the perspective of a dead person rather than a living one?

2. What words or phrases in "Go and catch a falling star" indicate that the speaker is not serious?

3. The speaker of "Go and catch a falling star" describes many impossible things. What is the connection between these impossible things and the poem's overall message?

4. What is similar about the messages of "Are you digging on my grave?" and "Go and catch a falling star"?

Connection Reflection

5. The speaker of "Are you digging on my grave?" guesses many people are digging on her grave, including her "enemy." However, the dog claims that the speaker's enemy does not care about her anymore. What does this reveal about the nature of rivalries? Do you think this is always the case?

6. In John Donne's time, many people wrote stories and songs about how women are never faithful in love. In "Go and catch a falling star," Donne makes fun of this popular theme. If you could make fun of a popular theme in your own culture, what would you choose? Why?

After you **read** a poem and **understand** its language, ask yourself, **what does it mean?**

Main Idea

Satire is a form of writing that uses humor, exaggeration, sarcasm, or ridicule in order to expose or critique a person, a people group, a concept, or society. Writers have often used satire to share their opinions about something in their social or political climate, usually something negative.

Gulliver's Travels by Jonathan Swift is an example of a lengthy, developed, and humorous satire. When Gulliver travels to the Kingdom of Lilliput, he encounters political parties who squabble over ridiculous things, such as the size of their boots' heels. Swift used this to satirize the political parties of England at the time (the Whigs and the Tories).

Both Hardy's and Donne's poems employ satire in their own way.

In "Are you digging on my grave?", what is Hardy satirizing? Provide elements in Hardy's poem that hint at what is satire.

POETRY

Day 4: After You Read

Writing Connection

One way rhyme scheme affects the mood of a poem is how it influences the rate at which a poem is read and which words are emphasized. An elongated, difficult rhyme scheme would not be a good choice for a humorous poem, just as a repetitive, bouncy rhyme scheme would not be fitting for a somber poem. When writing a poem with rhyme, one should be sure the rhyme scheme is appropriate for the subject matter.

Write a poem using the same rhyme scheme as "Are you digging on my grave?" by Thomas Hardy. Choose a topic that you think is appropriate for the rhyming pattern.

Breaking Boundaries

Sing for the People – John Donne wrote many songs that he would sing to groups of friends and acquaintances gathering in parlors. His poem "Go and catch a falling star" is one such song (the poem is labeled "Song" in Donne's notes). Set "Go and catch a falling star" to your own arrangement of music.

Literary History – John Donne was part of the Metaphysical poets of the seventeenth century, and Thomas Hardy was one of the Realist poets in the Victorian era. Research either the Metaphysicals or the British Realists (or both, if you wish) to learn the context in which these poets were writing.

One Art / How Do I Love Thee?

Day 1: Before You Read

WHAT TO LEARN?
- Symbolism
- Rhythm and Rhyme

Do HARD *things*

Have you ever felt the desire to do something difficult, like learn an intricate trick on your bicycle, play the highest level in a video game, or hike an advanced mountain trail? Performers and athletes often attempt difficult things. They challenge themselves to expand their abilities and accomplish more than they have before.

What is the benefit of doing difficult things?

By accomplishing something that does not come easily, people can hone their existing skills and develop new ones. For this reason, poets sometimes challenge themselves to write according to certain rules for rhythm and rhyme; that is, to adhere to fixed forms. Examples of fixed poetic forms include sonnets, epics, odes, villanelles, and heroic couplets.

Both Elizabeth Bishop and Elizabeth Barrett Browning wrote in fixed poetic forms.

Meet the Authors

American Literature

British Literature

Wide Travels, Sparse Writing

Elizabeth Bishop
Feb 8, 1911–Oct 6, 1979

As a child, Bishop lost her parents and had to live with her grandparents in Canada and Boston. After college, she spent time in France, Spain, North Africa, Ireland, Italy, Florida, and Brazil. She is considered a great American poet, but she published only 101 poems in her lifetime, for she was a perfectionist who refined her work until it was precise and meaningful.

More Than a Love Song

Elizabeth Barrett Browning
Mar 6, 1806–June 29, 1861

Browning is most famous for her love poetry, but her life is a fascinating study. She had a tyrannical father, wrote in favor of abolition (even though her family's wealth depended on slave labor), was physically disabled, carried on a secret courtship and elopement when she was forty years old (with fellow poet Robert Browning), personally knew many famous literary figures of her time, and achieved celebrity poet status herself.

POETRY 143

Analyzing Figurative Language — Symbolism

Symbolism is the use of a person, place, object, or action to express a deeper or double meaning, sometimes describing an idea or concept that has no physical attributes. Readers must utilize the context a poem provides, their own reasoning, and their knowledge of common symbols to discover symbolic meaning. "One Art" by Elizabeth Bishop uses many subtle symbols, as does "How Do I Love Thee?" by Elizabeth Barrett Browning.

Identify possible symbolic meanings for the symbols listed and one you find yourself. Explain your answers and indicate from which poem you identify the symbol.

Symbol	Symbolic Meaning	Explanation
A continent ("One Art")	A place overseas where the speaker spent time	*The speaker couldn't literally own an entire continent, like the poem says, but she could spend time there. The phrase symbolizes an important place on another continent that the poet had to leave (because she "lost" it).*

Analyzing Figurative Language activity provided in the Resource Book on page 136.

Element of Poetry: Rhythm and Rhyme

"One Art" is a villanelle, and "How Do I Love Thee?" is a sonnet; both are examples of **fixed forms** of poetry, but the sonnet is much more popular.

A **sonnet** has fourteen lines written in *iambic pentameter*, meaning every line has ten syllables divided into five sets of *iambs*—a certain pattern of stressed and unstressed syllables. Sonnets also follow a specific rhyme scheme and division of thought. An **Italian sonnet** divides its rhyme and content between an *octave* and a *sestet*, and an **English sonnet** divides its rhyme and content into three *quatrains* and a concluding *couplet*.

Use a slash (/) for unstressed syllables.

Use a carat (^) for stressed syllables.

Identifying the pattern of stressed and unstressed syllables in a poem is called **scanning**.

Scan each line of "How Do I Love Thee?" and record the rhyme scheme. Draw boxes around each main section of the poem, identifying whether the poem is an Italian sonnet or an English sonnet.

Element of Poetry activity provided in the Resource Book on page 138.

Read "One Art" by Elizabeth Bishop and "How Do I Love Thee?" by Elizabeth Barrett Browning

 Day 3: After You Read

Think About It

1. Both "One Art" and "How Do I Love Thee?" mention another person, a "you" or a "thee." Do you think both speakers are talking directly to the person they mention, or are the poems confessions to self rather than confessions to the "you"? Explain your answer.

2. What words or phrases in "One Art" create the somber, introspective mood of the poem?

3. What do you think the speaker of "How Do I Love Thee?" means when she (or he) says, "I love thee... / when feeling out of sight / for the ends of being and ideal grace"?

4. "How Do I Love Thee?" is a romantic poem; what about "One Art"? Is the "you" in the last stanza necessarily a romantic love? Why or why not?

Connection Reflection

5. "One Art" is not only about misplacing objects but also about being deprived of things that are important. In your experience, how does it feel to lose something important? Have you ever lost something important to you? Share your experience.

6. Do you think "How Do I Love Thee?" is an accurate description of true love? With what elements do you agree or disagree?

After you read a poem and understand its language, ask yourself, what does it mean?

Main Idea

Sometimes people process emotions or thoughts better when they put them down in writing. This process is called **catharsis**, meaning a release of emotions that causes relief.

A

How might "One Art" be an example of catharsis? Consider what the poet might have been feeling when she wrote the poem.

B

In the final line of "One Art," the poet intrudes into her own poem with: "(Write it!)" What does this intrusion reveal about how the poet felt?

POETRY 145

Day 4: After You Read

Writing Connection

Writing poetry in free verse can be a fun and perfect mode for self-expression, but writing a poem that obeys the rules of fixed forms can also be rewarding. Sometimes a certain topic or tone is best expressed in a fixed form. While it can be a challenge to craft one's words to fit a particular meter, rhyme scheme, or repeating pattern, doing so can result in a feeling of satisfied accomplishment.

Choose one of the topics listed (or one of your own thinking) and write a sonnet about the topic. If you are not able to accomplish the meter or rhyme scheme, at least match the division of thought. Remember, you can craft an Italian sonnet or an English sonnet.

Topics:
—your significant other
—the home you grew up in
—your favorite aspect of nature

> *Remember!*
>
> *A sonnet has fourteen lines written in iambic pentameter.*
>
> *An Italian sonnet divides its rhyme and content between an octave and a sestet.*
>
> *An English sonnet divides its rhyme and content into three quatrains and a concluding couplet.*

Breaking Boundaries

Lives from History – Elizabeth Barrett Browning's life was a rollercoaster of despair and joy. Research her life in the 1800s, especially the events that led to her famous love poetry.

Travel – Both Elizabeth Bishop and Elizabeth Barrett Browning traveled to different countries as well as different continents. If you could travel anywhere in the world, where would you go? Create a folder detailing your ideal travel plans, complete with important information about the locations as well as a wishlist of what you want to do.

Sing Me a Pop Song – Compare Browning's love poem to love songs written today. You may select songs from any musical genre. Consider what is similar or different about what is said or how it is said.

Having a Coke with You [in Just-]

Day 1: Before You Read

WHAT TO LEARN?
- Allusion
- Mood and Tone

A thousand fibers CONNECT us

When you think, speak, or do anything, is what you are doing an independent action formed entirely in your own brain, or are your actions and thoughts influenced by something outside of you? In other words, are you autonomous, or is everything you do connected to something or someone else?

Much of what we think and say is influenced by outside factors. A friend may start talking about your favorite movie, which influences you to give your opinion of it. A childhood experience may cause you to fear thunder, even though as an adult you understand that you are safe inside your home. Books, movies, and television shows can also be influential, spurring popular quotes or themes in other forms of art and media.

Brainstorm with your teacher or fellow classmates to come up with cultural connections you have encountered. Were they between you and another person, or were they somewhere else, such as in an advertisement or movie?

Meet the Authors

 American Literature

 American Literature

Frank O'Hara
Mar 27, 1926–July 25, 1966

The Poetry of People

O'Hara's biographers note that his poetry—urbane, innovative, and avant-garde—sounds like entries in a diary rather than formal pieces of literature. O'Hara himself felt that poetry should be "between two persons rather than two pages." He was the leader of the "New York School" of poets, a group that engaged with the worlds of music, dance, and painting, and he asserted that poetry could and should be mixed with other forms of art rather than being a separate entity.

e e cummings
Oct 14, 1894–Sep 3, 1962

Breaking All the Rules

Edward Estlin Cummings is recognized as one of the foremost avant-garde poets. He experimented with punctuation, spelling, syntax, and all forms of language to create poetry that did not adhere to convention but became an entirely new genre, prompting the reader to carefully consider what the author meant. The lack of capitalization and punctuation in his name is not an error; cummings preferred to stylize his name in such a manner.

POETRY 147

Day 2: Before You Read

Analyzing Figurative Language — Allusion

An **allusion** is a reference to something outside of a work, something the author assumes the reader will understand. The word "allusion" came to English from the Latin word *alludere*, which means "play toward." An allusion, then, is something that plays at (or toward) something else while integrating it into a new setting.

In literature, allusions are intentional stylistic choices authors make that suggest relationships between a work of literature and previous events in history or other works of art. In Edgar Allan Poe's "The Raven," the poem's narrator asks the titular bird if there is "balm in Gilead," an allusion not only to the biblical book of Jeremiah but also to the balm of Gilead as a symbol of universal healing.

Record allusions from O'Hara's "Having a Coke with You" and cummings' [in Just-]. Research what these allusions refer to and explain what they mean. List reasons for why you think the poet might have chosen to use these allusions.

Allusions	Explanations	Reasons
Travesera de Gracia ("Having a Coke with You")	The Travesera de Gracia (now known as the Travessera de Gracia) is a street in Barcelona that is named after Gracia, which is a district the street crosses.	O'Hara says that having a Coke is more fun than being sick to his stomach on this street, so maybe he was traveling while he was sick and is saying that having a Coke is more fun than that experience.

Analyzing Figurative Language activity provided in the Resource Book on page 140.

Element of Poetry: Mood and Tone

Mood refers to what the reader feels when reading a work of literature; conversely, **tone** refers to how the author of a piece feels about their subject. Mood and tone work together, for the author's tone influences the reader's mood. A humorous poem will likely evoke joy and happiness from the reader; a somber poem commemorating fallen soldiers will likely evoke sadness or despondency.

Identify the mood and tone of cummings' [in Just-]. Record each in the correct boxes and then explain why you think the poem displays the mood and tone you chose. Be sure to use details from the text to support your answer.

Element of Poetry activity provided in the Resource Book on page 142.

Read "Having a Coke with You" by Frank O'Hara and "[in Just-]" by e e cummings

 Day 3: After You Read

Think About It

1. Look back to your list of allusions found in "Having a Coke with You." What is the prevailing pattern in the things to which O'Hara is alluding, and why do you think O'Hara chose this pattern?

2. What does the speaker of "Having a Coke with You" mean when he says "and the portrait show seems to have no faces in it at all, just paint / you suddenly wonder why in the world anyone ever did them"?

3. Why do you think e e cummings chose to make the structure of [in Just-] different from the structure of a regular poem?

4. What do you think the speaker of [in Just-] means when he says the balloonman "whistles far and wee"?

Connection Reflection

5. Is there someone in your life (not necessarily a romantic interest) who makes you feel like O'Hara feels toward the subject of his poem? Do any of his descriptions or allusions describe how you feel about this person? If not, how would you describe your feelings?

6. Cummings creates words such as "puddle-wonderful" and "mudlicious" to describe spring. What words would you create to describe your favorite season?

After you **read** a poem and **understand** its language, ask yourself, **what does it mean?**

Main Idea

Both "Having a Coke with You" and [in Just-] use allusions, but the way they use allusions is different: O'Hara's poem is composed almost entirely of allusions while cummings' poem makes one primary allusion.

In "Having a Coke with You," who is the speaker's audience? What is the speaker trying to say to his audience through his many allusions?

B

What is the topic of [in Just-], and how does its allusion factor into the poem?

POETRY

Day 4: After You Read

Writing Connection

Allusions, like other forms of figurative language, strengthen poetry. They connect it to other works of literature and pieces of culture and share this deeper meaning with the reader. When noticed, allusions create a relationship between the reader and the poem or the reader and the author who chose to use these allusions.

Write a poem about something important to you—a person, an event, or a belonging—that uses at least two allusions to help describe the importance of your poem's subject or the way you view it. If you wish, you may imitate O'Hara and cummings by writing in free verse, or you may write a more traditional poem.

Breaking Boundaries

Fine Arts – Research the numerous works of art to which O'Hara alludes in his poem "Having a Coke with You." Read about the inspiration behind them, the artists who created them, and how they have been received by art critics.

The Music of Poetry – Set the words of either "Having a Coke with You" or [in Just-] to music, paying special attention to the rhythm of the poem you choose. What genre of music is most appropriate for each poem? What instruments fit the mood and tone of the poem? If you wish, you may rearrange or remove portions of the poem in order to create your song.

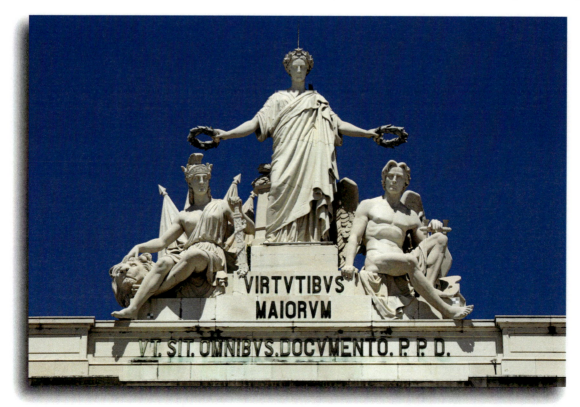

Complete Poetry Unit Summative Assessment

Poetry Summative Assessment is provided in the Resource Book on page 144.